Father Time

Father Time

Stories on the Heart and Soul of Fathering

Christopher Scribner, PhD

Chris Frey, MSW

Insight Output
Training and Publications
St. Louis

Insight Output
Training and Publications
P.O. Box 1944
St. Louis, MO 63043

©2001 Christopher Scribner and Chris Frey

Cover design by Lilyann Rice / In Graphic Detail

Cataloging-in-Publication Data
Scribner, Christopher.
  FatherTime : stories on the heart and soul of fathering / Christopher Scribner, Chris Frey – 1st ed.
    p. cm.
    LCCN: 00-105245
    ISBN: 0-9702610-0-4

  1. Fatherhood. 2. Father and child. 3. Fathers.
4. Parenting. I. Frey, Chris L. II. Title.

HQ756.S36 2000   306.874'2
                                  QBI00-863

 PRINTED IN CANADA

To Daniel and Abby, who accept my love and tolerate my shortcomings; to Susan, who has fostered the growth of my children since before I even met them; and to my father and grandfathers, for loving their children.

C.S.

To Harold Frey; my father ... my friend.

C.F.

ABOUT THE AUTHORS

Chris Frey, MSW, LCSW, is a retreat leader, writer, and psychotherapist in private practice in St. Louis, Missouri. Frey has gained national recognition for his work in men's issues, sexual addiction, and sexual abuse recovery. He is the author of **Men At Work: An Action Guide To Masculine Healing** and **Double Jeopardy: Treating Juvenile Victims And Perpetrators For The Dual Disorder Of Sexual Abuse And Substance Abuse** (Islewest Publishing); his poetry has also been published in several journals. He has served as clinical consultant to both sexual abuse and chemical dependency treatment programs, and was the author of the Sexual Abuse and Substance Abuse Program (SASAP) pioneered at Boy's Town of Missouri. Frey is a frequent presenter on a national level to both lay and professional audiences in the areas of men's work and sexuality. He is the father of Carly, Aimee, and Nathan, and husband of DiAnne.

Christopher Scribner, PhD, is a Phi Beta Kappa graduate of Earlham College who completed his training in Clinical Psychology at the University of Tennessee. In the past, he's been an intercollegiate Ultimate Frisbee® player, a clinical faculty member in a medical school psychiatry department, a wedding photographer, psychological consultant for a theater production, director of a Rehabilitation Psychology division in a large urban hospital, and a psychotherapist. Re-balancing his priorities, he chose to leave the world of clinical practice and now devotes his energies to teaching, writing, and fathering. His prose and poetry have appeared in an eclectic mix of humor, professional, and literary publications, including *Satire, Journal of Irreproducible Results, Psychotherapy Bulletin, Journal of Personality Assessment*, and *Parenting Network*. He is also a regular contributor to *Light: The Quarterly of Light Verse*, where his work has been praised as "inspired; showing nimble wit, verve, and invention." Dr. Scribner lives in St. Louis, Missouri with his wife Susan, his daughter Abby, and his son Daniel.

. CONTENTS .

TALES FROM THE TRENCHES

       Eight stories about the ways in which fatherhood challenges the father to examine himself and his priorities, thereby offering opportunities for him to grow along with his child

       Up There • *Absent Fathers* • *Father's Day* • *Confronting Dad* • *Whose Eyes* • *Working, Playing* • *Picking Up Baby* • *Follow-Up There*

FOREWORD

Here is a book for parents and parents-to-be who seek to strengthen the role of healthy fathers in the lives of children. Chris Scribner and Chris Frey have crafted 52 stories, 52 opportunities for men and women to be inspired, educated, and challenged toward a greater understanding of the art of fathering. Chris and Chris both carry into this book their extensive experience as psychotherapists, teachers and retreat leaders. However, the true beauty of **FatherTime** is that these men are coming to us first and foremost as fathers and sons, sharing their hearts with us and only then offering the benefit of their professional insights. These men highlight a broad spectrum of issues in fathering by sharing the lessons gleaned from their own on-the-job training.

I first became aware of Chris Frey's work in 1997 through his book, **Men At Work: An Action Guide to Masculine Healing**, which reflected a deep commitment to developing models for healthy masculinity. In **FatherTime**, his passionate and practical approach is joined by the ringing clarity and heart-felt evocativeness of Chris Scribner's voice. In unison, they offer inspiration, and they challenge men to reach deep to achieve their full potential as fathers.

Like parenting itself, the stories in this book are by turns poignant, joyous, sharp-edged, and funny. They show and acknowledge mistakes, and report and build upon successes. I encourage you to let yourself be drawn in as these stories echo and amplify your own particular life experiences. Ponder the wonder and fear of childbirth, the grief of a father's death, weaning a toddler from the pacifier, a teenager's first date. Enter the world of the father and child through squirt guns, bicycling, baseball gloves, divorce, and remarriage. And, perhaps most importantly in a culture where men often struggle in isolation and disconnection, each story invites you to step further into the world of common experience shared by fathers.

In much of my own writing, I describe what boys need to become strong, responsible, sensitive men. Physically, emotionally, and spiritually present fathers provide an essential cornerstone in the development of boys and girls. As you proceed through **FatherTime**, you will encounter fathers and mentors who are such men. I trust you will be enlightened by the honesty, strength, humanity, and wit contained in these pages. I hope you will be energized by Chris and Chris, and awakened to a more conscious type of fathering in your own life. Best wishes on your journey.

-- Michael Gurian, author of **The Wonder of Boys** and **A Fine Young Man**

INTRODUCTION

Dear fellow fathers:

This book is for you, the good fathers everywhere who desire to go deeper into the joy and passion of fathering. This is not a technical book filled with data on child development; good books like that are already available elsewhere. This is a book about HEART, about going inside – inside of YOU – to discover the best father you can be ... and to discover what keeps you, at times, from being that man. This is a book about taking it to the next level.

Through these stories, you will find a way to plumb the true depths of your love for your children. You may become more comfortable with the job at hand. The adventurers among you will use these pages to transcend that troublesome, nagging issue that trips you up repeatedly in dealing with your kids – whether it's perfectionism, control, anger, impatience, or some other aspect of your personality that you'll soon discover.

You will interpret these stories in your own way; you will find your own personal meaning in each; some will touch you more than others. You will have the opportunity to act on the knowledge that you could be more of a presence in the lives of your children ... physically, emotionally, spiritually.

Read on.

With hope,
Chris and Chris

CHRIS FREY'S STORY:

I began these writings without any intention of publication; my stories were a diary of sorts, an effort to encapsulate my evolution as a father and establish a series of guideposts that might prod me in my continuing journey toward becoming an even better dad. I was pleased with what I found: renewed memories of the gifts I received from my parents and other father figures, moments frozen in time that remind me of my best fathering, perspectives on insecurities and inadequacies that challenge me even to this day.

Why, then, did I eventually choose to put these writings in book form? I came to believe that what I was writing was an Everyman story; one of love and wounding, one of closeness and absence, one of misguided effort and perfect moments, a story that would mirror the experiences of many other men. I had parented my children through two marriages, and, in between, as a single father. I had gained much of the technical data of parenting that I had lacked as a new father who was inexperienced in caring for children. I had felt deep love and gained a reputation as a good father. Yet, as my daughters, Carly and Aimee, moved through adolescence and my son, Nathan, arrived, I was awakened by a deeper need. This need is best described as a desire to re-learn fathering from the inside out ... less data and more soul-searching. This is what brought me to masculine healing work, in my

4

career, in my life. Improving as a father became my most important emotional and spiritual process.

And so, through my writings I came to believe that I might ignite a spark in you, the reader, a desire to look toward the inner journey of your fathering experience, or the experience of a father close to you. This means looking as deeply at how we have been fathered as at how we father. This means working from a foundation of introspection and action, an intention captured in an old Native American saying: Life can only be understood *backwards*, but it can only be lived *forwards*. This book is about that truth, healing and honoring the past as a method to be better dads today. It works.

So, I began to think "book" as I continued writing my stories. And what to my wondering eyes should appear but Chris Scribner, a friend, colleague and fellow writer, who in casual conversation shared that he'd been writing brief stories on his fathering experiences for a while. More than coincidence.

CHRIS SCRIBNER'S STORY:

I came from a big family. I had a lot of exposure to babies, and witnessed a lot of care-taking, all from a young age. I was brought up by my parents, but also to varying degrees by my eight older siblings. I saw an endless parade of young nieces and nephews being cared for by their young parents, my eldest siblings. I began my hands-on

5

experience with holding, feeding, and burping babies around the age of 9 or 10.

The prospect of becoming a father never terrified me; I was confident that I could handle the basic requirements of the job. But at a certain point in my growth as a father, I realized that I wanted more, and that my children deserved more. And I realized that providing them with what I felt they deserved required growth on my part – not growth in "parenting skills," that catch-phrase that describes the technical side of parenting, but growth in *myself* – especially in my capacity to feel, show, and share joy.

This realization took on particular urgency with the birth of my second child – a son. I'd been a father for several years, and was comfortable with how I'd been doing as a father to my daughter, Abby. But when Daniel was born – when I became father to a son – it occurred to me that it was crucial for me to find my passion as a father, if I was to be the father my son deserved. I found myself thinking more and more about my own father, who died when I was 14. He was a good man, a capable and caring father, and a man whose emotions were characteristically muted – a style, no doubt, which was often an asset in his efforts to rear ten children, but also a style which I took on to such an extent that it interfered with my capacity to experience more intense emotions. As I looked ahead to my life as a father I saw myself becoming, like him, a low-keyed, muted, competent, caring father. Without doubt, my children would be well-cared-for and capably-taken-care-of. But I wanted to offer them more than that, and the main thing standing in my way was my habit of focusing on competence at the expense of joy and passion. I knew that, for me, joy and passion were the qualities that would allow me to become the father I wanted to be.

So I invested myself in personal-growth work. Through this work I got to know Chris Frey, and when we realized that we'd been working independently on very similar writing projects, we decided to collaborate on this book. United by our commitment to finding the joy in fathering, we wrote and fathered, fathered and wrote. Eventually, we had compiled enough of our own stories that we thought we'd share them with like-minded fathers.

In the writing of **FatherTime**, we have lived what we are attempting to teach; these writings encompass several years in our journeys as growing dads. As you read, we hope you receive some of the gifts we found in writing. Read and ponder the stories. Discuss them; write in your journal about them. If you wish to go deeper, consider seeking the assistance of significant others or a circle of men to glean the gold from these pages. You may even use **FatherTime** as a format for healing work with a men's group or in therapy. Do what you need to do. Do what you can.

OUR FATHERS

In early discussions about the book, we developed the plan to present our thoughts on the importance of fathers. As we began writing, though, we realized that you already *know* how important your father is. You know by virtue of what you got from him that was valuable or important to you, and you know by virtue of the void that was left by what you *didn't* get from him. Either way, or in both ways, you know.

You know because he taught you how to ride a bike, mow the lawn, catch a trout, plant a garden, tell a joke, or balance a checkbook. You know because he died too young, or drank too much, or got too angry, or traveled too much on his job. You know your father's importance because he hugged, hit, spoke, listened, stayed, ran away. You are connected at a gut level to the understanding that the space this man filled, or the void he left, has been instrumental in shaping the person you've become; you feel it every day.

If you're able to admire your father, this knowledge is a source of great comfort, even joy. To this day, you may sit with your dad over coffee, retelling old family tales; you may work side by side, or care for his physical needs as his health declines, or seek his advice on matters of importance. If this is your story, you and your father are truly blessed.

On the other hand, you may know of the power of this influence by the pain you feel at its absence. You may be a paternal patchwork quilt, of sorts, shaped by the hands of too many dads: biological, adoptive, step; men who came and went from mother's life. You may be one of the many who never met dad, or have no memory of him, sitting with the ache in your soul created by an almost indescribable loss. Perhaps your father was stolen from you by death or by the unjust decision of some misguided divorce judge or mother. Or maybe he simply wasn't very good at the job at hand, fathering. The pain you feel may be quiet, barely discernible through the noise of, "I'm nothing like my dad; I didn't even know him." Or, the wound may have a sound like crashing cymbals: "I hated him ... he's nothing to me ... I had no father." If this is your story, healing these wounds could be your blessing, and the blessing you will give the children that you bring into this world. For without such healing you will surely repeat many of the mistakes of the man you deny. Your father's legacy echoes within you; it appears in your physical features, your temperament, your strengths, your shortcomings. That's where it begins for every son who becomes a father; it can be no other way. Inadequacies in fathering have a way of repeating themselves, generation after generation, until the generation arrives when a man steps out to proclaim "This needs to stop, and *I* will stop it."

<u>DADS</u>

Each of us has only one father, one man with weaknesses and strengths, who lent his fertility to one woman and gave us our beginning. The *father* role is defined biologically. The role of *dad*, on the other hand, is conferred by the children, and refers to the man or men who occupy the sacred place of "man who holds great emotional significance in my life." The title of *dad* may be given to one's biological father, but may just as well be given to another man. Not every father is a dad, and not every dad is a father.

Some of you have only one dad -- that biological father who gave you your earthly jump-start and then stuck around to love and teach and make human mistakes while practicing on you. Others of you have the mixed blessing of multiple dads, men who did not bring you into this world, yet made the choice to become a part of your life through adoption, or partnering with mom. Many of these men care, deeply, without the benefit of a blood connection. Countless men tell stories like these:

> "I have two dads. When mom remarried, my step-dad accepted us as his children, but he never tried to replace our father."

> "I know I have a biological father, but I don't know anything about him. My dad is simply my dad; he raised me,

loved me; I never heard him call me his 'adopted child.'"

"It was hard when mom divorced again. My step-dad and I were close; he was like my real dad."

These men, these *dads,* are heroes.

But not all memories of dads are of safety, acceptance, and love. Many of us carry dad wounds right alongside our father wounds. Perhaps you carry memories of too many dads, of men who claimed your mother but denied you, of men who fooled the adoption agency by concealing their inability to parent you well in your second chance at having a dad. Read on.

FATHER FIGURES

And then there are the father figures: grandfathers, uncles, coaches, neighbors, teachers, Scout leaders; strong, benevolent, compassionate men who mentor our children into manhood and womanhood.

Chris Frey's story:

I remember we had moved for the first time. I was 12 years old, in a new state, a new town, a new school. Dad was re-starting his career after years in the family business; we both recall that he was gone from home much of the time. Across the street was the White family. Foss was a Scout leader; I was a reluctant Scout in another troop. It was winter and somehow, I don't recall exactly how, Foss tendered an offer for me to go hiking with him in the Michigan woods. I accepted and there we were, walking through the bright white snow, surrounded by pines and ... tracking deer. I remember being quiet; I remember following Foss' lead, walking carefully, kneeling to examine the deer tracks, pretending I understood the meaning of this experience. After a time, Foss held up his hand. We stopped, stooped down, peered through an opening in the evergreens, and gazed at a wondrous, elegant doe. We stayed in that position for I don't remember how long and watched -- no camera, no guns, only our eyes to record the moment.

I did not reflect on this day for many years, not until, in my adulthood, I began to look at the gifts I had received from men in my life who were not in my bloodline. In this reflection I found I had imprinted a powerful perception in the hushed recesses of my consciousness ... there are men, mentors, who will have time for me ... there are men, older men, who will know I struggle and reach out. I know that this insight, tucked away, left me open to the future influence of Jack Parkhurst, Grafton Hull, Bob Brundage, Stefan Rybak, Jim Howard, even my own father; all men who would come into my life during times of confusion, all men who would become guides through the woods of the future.

<u>Chris Scribner's story:</u>

I lost my father before I became a man, but I've been blessed with numerous men who have served as father figures, mentors, in my life. Many of them appeared in my life between the ages of 18 and 26, years that I spent in school -- and years that I was struggling to find myself as a person and as a man.

I extend the largest portion of gratitude to Dale Noyd -- my teacher, my mentor, who took me under his wing and treated me as "special" when that was exactly what I was needing. Dale recognized and trumpeted my intellectual gifts; modeled that incisive, renegade thinking style, and taught me much about zeal and passion.

But numerous other men served as father figures for me as well. In my youth there was Ken Holian, coach and fatherly presence, who politely overlooked my limitations as a hitter and instead made a big deal out of my grace in the field as a second-baseman (introducing me to the phrase "poetry in motion"). Len Handler, teacher, male-mother who warmly accepted my insecurities and thereby helped me to do the same. Pete Watrous, who helped me find just enough arrogance to neutralize my self-doubts; and Ron DeMao, veteran of life, who provided low-keyed but invaluable guidance along multiple paths at an important time of transition in my life. And, more lately, two very fatherly figures: Bernie Steinberg, who has known me only as a fellow man and treats me as such; and John Mella, whom I know only through the mails, who has given blessings and encouragement to my creativity.

Fathers, dads, and father-figures all influence our views of ourselves as sons. Just as importantly, though, they shape the kind of father we become.

OURSELVES

We've acknowledged the importance of our fathers, dads, and father figures. What about ourselves as fathers?

These days, fatherhood can take any number of shapes; the traditional configuration of steady, responsible breadwinner who holds a job, brings home a paycheck, and occasionally metes out a bit of "discipline" to his children (who are, after all, mainly their *mother's* responsibility) is becoming increasingly rare.

Chances are, that doesn't describe *your* situation. As a father, you're more likely striving to be a true co-parent, sharing the parenting role with your children's mother in ways that are equal or complementary. The challenges are magnified when, as is often true, both of you also work. This juggling of roles – career person, spouse/ex-spouse, *and* parent – necessitates a great deal of flexibility from both of you. For you, it may entail stepping into unfamiliar roles and applying skills that are largely untested.

Or you may belong to that growing minority of men, the single father. As a single father, you may face special challenges. First, our culture barely recognizes that you exist. There is a myth that virtually all single parents are female ... not so. Second, just as wonderful single mothers cannot be both man and woman, neither can the single dad. We honor those of you who are in this role, who choose to stay involved with your children. And we honor those of you who do even more than that, and become the primary caretaker.

A PHILOSOPHY OF FATHERING

We believe that fathers and dads are the most vital influence on our children's views of men and masculinity. This is true in spite of the myriad of views offered to our children from outside the family by the media, by peers, or via the Internet. This is true in spite of our high divorce rate. It's true in spite of the western cultural myth that no child over the age of 12 will value a close parent-child relationship (at least until he or she reaches adulthood and realizes how truly wise we were in our parenting). We believe that our loving presence is the primary rudder which guides our children toward the sense of healthy masculinity that we hope to bequeath to them.

In the media, opinions abound on the topic of what's wrong with fathers. Some such criticisms are valid. But more helpful would be efforts to define explicitly what fathering should be. Many men do best when they have a clearly-articulated goal to reach for. This is why we are offering our attempt to define several key principles of fathering.

of fathering. Some of these were first offered in Chris Frey's book **Men at Work: An Action Guide to Masculine Healing**.   Others emerged from the stories that follow. Taken together, they serve as the framework for our view of fathering.

♦**As a father, I will be a "presence" in the lives of my children** – this implies a commitment to making a positive emotional impact on my children. Financial responsibility comes into play here, but I also need to know that being a "good provider" entails more than money and material things. If circumstances demand frequent physical absence, I must take steps to ensure my ongoing presence within the household in symbolic ways, to maintain the emotional connection with my children.

♦**As a father, I will be self-aware** – aware of my strengths and weaknesses as a parent, aware of my unresolved issues, aware of my areas of vulnerability, aware of my unique gifts and talents as a father, and aware enough to be able to distinguish my emotional "stuff" from my child's emotional "stuff."

♦**As a father, I will find the joy in fathering** – that is, doing something more than "going through the motions." For many of us, finding the joy in fathering requires that we expand our ability to experience joy more generally – which may take some work.

♦**As a father, I will provide a safe haven for my children** – if children do not feel safe in their relationship with their father, they are at risk to feel unsafe in the world more generally. A father provides limits and guidance in the service of creating a safe "container" in which his children can grow and learn. Part of the father's role is to create a psychological space in which the children feel free to be who they are – *all* aspects of who they are; and feel free to express their feelings – *all* of their feelings.

♦**As a father, I will honor the presence and importance of the mother of my children** – just as my interactions with my children influence their view of themselves, my interactions with their mother will influence their view of male-female relationships. Caring, mutuality, and respect must be evidenced in my actions toward her and in my reactions to her efforts as co-parent. This applies regardless of whether we are together, divorced, or never married.

♦**As a father, I will model accountability and integrity** – these two are easy to define, challenging to model. Being accountable means taking full responsibility for one's actions, choices, and decisions. The person who is being accountable does not seek to assign blame and, if victimized, does not permanently adopt the victim role. Instead, he lives courageously, accepting and affirming that he is in charge of his actions, and accepting that every act and every choice he makes will have consequences, which he also accepts courageously. Living with integrity means saying what you truly mean and truly meaning what you say. One's words and actions are congruent. The person living with integrity does not say one thing, then do another. He does not search for the loopholes, does not employ linguistic or emotional sleight-of-hand, does not evade the truth. This, too, is a courageous way of living.

Throughout **FatherTime**, you will find stories that reflect the challenge of **being present**, at times for great celebrations, but mostly for the simple daily stuff that builds trust and closeness. You will find examples of the struggle and satisfaction of gaining and maintaining the level of **self-awareness** that fathering well requires. You will find tales about the **joy of fathering**, the fun within the job. You will read about providing **safety and security** and protection, features of fathering that are too often in short supply. You will find stories that encourage you to look at your relationship with **your children's mother**, and to honor her contributions to their lives. And you will find tales of the wide range of opportunities that fathers have to embrace and model **personal integrity and accountability**, once we're on the lookout for them; they appear in play, in work, in crisis, in the mundane.

As you read the stories, we hope you'll reflect on them, and ask whether they contain something that might be relevant to your own functioning as a father. The usefulness of this book is determined by the extent to which it inspires new perspectives or understandings in you, and the extent to which it creates new opportunities for action on your part.

Make **FatherTime** your book. Start now.

THE CHALLENGE

Each child is an adventure into a better life—an opportunity to change the old pattern and make it new.

-- Hubert H. Humphrey

1

UP THERE

(Scribner)

♦

This week, for the first time, I hoist my infant son over my head so he can ride on the back of my neck. He's wildly amused to be up there. When he gives his blissful shimmy, I feel a wave of panic. What if I drop him? Am I strong enough, steady enough to support him? Should I restrain his joyous gesticulating, as I feel my own was restrained during my youth? If not, how shall I master my own fearfulness?

Like fathers everywhere, I hoist him to give him the advantage of my height. This is part of fathering: the child reaping the benefits of what the father has attained. After a slow start, I've attained the height of six feet. Presently, that's an advantage of 44 inches over my son, so I lend him my tallness.

In seven years, I will lend him my old baseball glove. In 12, it will be my sweatshirts. In 15, my car. In 20, my sage thoughts on marriage. In 25, the grudging lessons gleaned from my mistakes in the work world.

In 30 years, God willing, we'll be talking about parenting. I'll try to show him the safe, firm grip I've perfected for carrying a baby on the back of my neck. My son will insist upon doing it in his own, more carefree way. And I, God willing, will smile, unafraid.

For another part of fathering is the child inspiring the father to resume growing.

2

ABSENT FATHERS

(Frey)

♦

I have heard it said in many circles that our world suffers from an epidemic of absent fathers, and no doubt this is true. Divorce, addictions, workaholism, death, corporate culture, and materialism have robbed many families of the daily physical, emotional, and spiritual presence of dad. How important is this information? It is critical:

> *Close your eyes for a moment ... breathe ... now, imagine a world without adult males ... boys are born and begin to grow ... one day, shortly after reaching manhood they simply disappear ... no one can explain exactly why they went away. The sons are gone ... what would be missing from the lives of daughters? What would be missing from the lives of sons? What would be missing from the lives of women? Feel the importance of your answers ... breathe and slowly open your eyes.*

What are the wounds created by the lack of a loving masculine presence? For the sons: Manhood is defined by what's missing, not what's available.

The boy is left with only a woman's definition of what a man is and can be. There is no one to moderate the powerful feminine energy, particularly in adolescence as the boy prepares for independence. Men are seen as liabilities. Deep grief is covered by anger and, often, apathy. For the daughters: There is no role model for what a husband or partner can be. The girl suffers confusion, anger, deep grief, fear about men. She vacillates between *depending on* men and *taking care of* men. There is no one to moderate the mother energy. For mothers: There may be some relief at the loss of a poor relationship, followed by the strain of far too much responsibility for raising the child (especially in these times when many of our extended family and community supports have also broken down).

Am I over-dramatizing? When I first considering writing the brief imagery you just experienced in preparation for a workshop on absent fathers, the concept of all men simply disappearing after they brought children into this world seemed a bit extreme. Then, I reflected again on my own experience as a son, a father and a therapist: my divorce and devotion to work, evaluating men in jail, counseling addicts, the uneducated and naïve acceptance of custody agreements by many divorcing men I have known. In reviewing my work and my life, it became clear that by intention and by ignorance many fathers live spending considerable time in two emotional states with regard to their children ... love and regret.

I have spoken of these beliefs in heartfelt conversations with my own father. Dad often worked six or seven days a week, with his labor providing me opportunities in education and lifestyle that he and mom never had. He was making his way in the man's world as he understood it. I appreciated him and I missed him. He was doing what he believed was right for me and Lisa and Kevin. And he has regrets. Realizing from the sharing our truths that our time together is not over, dad and I have acted on these regrets. Each of us has listened to the other man's memories, thoughts and feelings. Then, we took the most important step: we became friends.

As for my own fathering, dad knows that through a divorce, my career, and a certain amount of emotional vacancy I have, at times, also been less than a fully present father. As part of every good father's quest to teach his son not to make the mistakes he made, dad has more than once cautioned me to keep my priorities straight and attend to my relationships with Carly, Aimee and Nathan. I have heeded his warning; I have improved and still am improving.

As I write this, I believe there are men who are saying, "What do you know, Chris ... my ex won't let me see my kids ... my kids don't want to see me ... my kids don't like my new partner ... my kids only want to talk to me when they want something ... I don't even know where my kids are." I honor all these obstacles as very real for many men. I can name good men whose ex-wives unjustly create distance between children and father because of their own unresolved baggage. Are you such a man? Because, if you are, I can also name good men who are taking action. If you are a conscientious father being kept from your children, there are excellent fathers' rights organizations that advocate for men who are unjustly being distanced from their kids; there are attorneys who specialize in this work; there are men of courage fighting the gender biases of the court system every day.

I also honor that some of the men who will read this story work six or seven days a week not only to give their children opportunities, such as my father, but perhaps to simply survive; to provide food and shelter. If you are such a father, whom do you call on as male mentors and elders, as teachers and life coaches? You do not have to be the only masculine resource for your children. You do not have to be alone.

For some men another question must be answered ... if you are being kept from your children, is there any good reason for that? Are they safe with you? Do you have the skills to adequately care for them, physically, emotionally, spiritually? If not, what are you doing about that? I know men who have lost touch with their children and years later re-established contact and loving relationships. I know men who expend large amounts of time and energy maintaining relationships with children from previous partners (often with the assistance of current partners). I know men, married and divorced, who go to therapy and workshops and retreats to learn the skills of translating the love they feel in their hearts into the actions of healthy fathering. I know men who have sobered up, paroled out, un-violenced and re-entered their children's' lives. I know a man whose children were taken out of the state, with the permission of the courts; he works hard to continue his relationship with them.

And, much less dramatic, I have known hundreds, maybe thousands, of men who simply get up each day with the intention of being awake, alive and present in the lives of their children. They fix lunches, carpool, play basketball, barbecue, become Cub Scout Leaders, help with homework, videotape every family event under the sun. And, often when it is toward the end of the day and this father is exhausted, he finds joy in reading a bedtime story and giving a goodnight kiss.

That's what I'm aiming for, men. Not for perfection. Not for being an all-knowing sage who makes no mistakes. I seek to be a man who wakes up and makes a conscious decision to be an active father every day; a man who decides to work on my issues, a man who communicates to the best of my ability with the mothers of my children; A MAN who doesn't attempt to accomplish these lofty goals on my own, but instead seeks out other men and women of wisdom as teachers for myself and mentors for my brood.

Speaking of which, it's time to go. I'm leaving work early and taking Nathan out of school. My buddy Jim Howard is taking Nathan and me down to march in the St. Patrick's day parade with the graduates of the all-boys high school he attended some 40+ years ago. A little marching, a little corned beef, and a lot of missing school and work. Excellent.

3

FATHER'S DAY

(Scribner)

♦

Having at long last the opportunity to sleep in, I lolled around in bed, fantasizing about the multitude of ways I would be honored on this Father's Day. I recalled the solemn promise from my often contentious daughter Abby, and looked forward to hearing her say "okay, Deeda" a minimum of twenty times today. My heart warmed as I thought of my toddler son Daniel running across the room, flinging himself against me in one of those whole-heart-and-soul hugs, then staying by my side throughout the day, wondrously watching my every move. Eventually, my yearning for those joys overcame my recumbent self-indulgence. I rolled out of bed, strode to the top of the stairs, paused for a moment with feet planted wide and hands on hips, and braced myself for the imminent glory as I prepared to descend into the warm, welcoming bosom of my family.

"No! Go away! Go away! Go away!" These loving words greeted me, issued from the mouth of Susan, the woman whose womb made me a father. My sleepy glimpse revealed to me only that she and my daughter – the child whose birth first conferred upon me the status of fatherhood – were working on some project, presumably meant for me on this hallowed day. Respectfully, I retreated to the kitchen to make a cup of coffee. The adoration would come soon, I was sure.

Hearing the sound of thick little footsteps, I turned around and fixed my eyes on the thirsty toddler approaching me. "Mo' bup?" he said, gesturing with the sippy-cup he held with both hands. Seizing this opportunity for interaction, I deferred his request and engaged him in conversation.

"You want some more milk to drink?"

"Sheah," he affirmed.

"Okay; give your cup to Daddy and I will fill it up for you."

"No." Solemn and firm. "No Daddy do. *Mommy* do."

"Well I think Mommy is busy right now, so Daddy will be happy to fill it up for you."

"Nooooooooo!" As the piercing sound escalated, I looked around to see if someone actually *was* strangling the cat. "*Mommy do! Mommy do!*" my son cried as he high-tailed it back to the family room.

Such was the inauspicious beginning to this Father's Day.

Before long I did get to see the card that my daughter was finishing up as I walked in, done with rainbow colors, flowers, and hearts galore. And I did get that enthusiastic toddler hug after my son had quenched his thirst with that special milk poured by *mother's* hand. And I got an appreciative hug, card, and thoughtful gift from Susan. She also gave me time to do yard work for a few hours, so I'd feel like the day had been "productive"; she realizes that's important to me these days.

But all in all the day was much like other days – making lunches; breaking up squabbles; snatching bits of conversation with my wife amidst all the reading, admiring, assisting, admonishing, cautioning, and nose-wiping interactions with the kids. This all reminded me of what being a father is all about. I was sad only for a moment that there wasn't more of a fuss being made in my honor, and noticed only in passing that my daughter didn't make it to 20 uncontested agreements with me. Then I went about celebrating Father's Day in the most fitting way of all: by *fathering* – doing the work, and doing it consciously and mindfully.

I found some dignity and honor in the drudgery of it all, and found some joy in those moments of appreciation or gratification – feeling my son's utter confidence in me as he brings me a broken toy to put back together; noticing his blossoming vocabulary; seeing my daughter's "I know you're just being silly" smile when I playfully toss absurdities in her direction.

Near the end of the day, I realized that I had not had a single thought of my own father on this day. He's been dead for 20 years, and it's not unusual for me to go through a day without thinking of him. But on this day it seemed significant, in a very positive way. You see, I've spent most of my adult years feeling more like a boy than a man, more like a kid than an adult, more like a son than a father. But on this day, set aside to honor fathers, I did not feel in the least like a son. On this day, and more and more days lately, I was a father, an adult, a man. It's as if I've claimed that title, and hold it more firmly than ever before.

I do wish my father were here to see it. But I'm glad my children's father is here, and glad too that they get to see him holding that title aloft, with more confidence today than yesterday, and with perhaps less than tomorrow.

4

CONFRONTING DAD

(Frey)

◆

My dad is a cool guy. He bought me my first basketball. He gave me the gifts of jazz and golf. He took me to The Factory, his place of work, and told me epic tales of the process of manufacturing stuffed animals; followed by huge burgers and heavenly malts at Behren's Drug Store. Much later in life, he also gave me the exact advice I needed to take my most frightening and most rewarding career risk, entering private therapy practice.

Perhaps the most powerful moment with dad in my conscious recall, however, occurred when I was into my 30's, and came not on the heels of these special times, but, instead, was drawn from my sad and angry memories of an imperfect father-son relationship:

Not only do I teach the healing of childhood pain, I walk the road myself and in the course of my journey I arrived at my time for a son's version of the Father-Son Talk; time to share with dad my truth about the best and worst of times in our history together. I had recently returned from a men's' workshop and endeavored to write dad a letter; my feelings about what I perceived as our long standing loving distance, a distance that I felt had, in some ways, left me woefully unprepared as a man, husband, and (with the impending birth of another child) father. I had information and feelings to share with my father and I hoped he had information and feelings that I still needed to hear. I followed the letter with a request to speak face-to-face with dad about these issues, not an opportunity for accusation or recrimination, but a time of making peace with my past.

So, several months later, there we were, just the two of us, talking about his childhood, and mine, his adulthood, and mine. We ate and talked for a long time, two of my favorite pastimes.

Over the years I have helped hundreds of clients prepare for similar conversations, but from all of my personal and professional experience, I could not have scripted a more healing slice of time with dad. Did he say everything I wanted him to, exactly as I had imagined? No. Did he agree with each of my perceptions, feelings, judgments? No. What he did do was openly listen to me and, then, share the story of being my father from his vantage point, his truth. He gave me information about himself I did not have. He corrected misconceptions I had about choices he had made. He owned his absences and many of his mistakes. And, when he told me he was proud of me, I felt his love course through me entire being, I believed him down to my socks ... into my soul. Then, my dad proved to be even more wise and crafty than I had ever given him credit for. As I remember, he mirrored back to me words that I have, in some version, shared with client after client after client as a teaching story ... In a moment so powerful I sometimes doubt it, he said, "So, if I had it to do all over again, Chris, I'd do some things differently. But, I'm not going to grow old feeling guilty, and if you're still angry at me, you're an adult and that's your stuff to work out." Boom!

My knee-jerk reaction was smoldering rage: he was obviously *not* repentant enough! My second, less jerky reaction was acceptance: my father had said to me *exactly* what I would say to a man (the key word being Man, not boy) working on his father wounds in therapy.

In the months that followed, my life began to make more sense to me. I was moving through my remaining boyhood and boyish struggles with a deeper understanding of the notion that being a son no longer held dominance over being a father, husband, a man. I began approaching my work, my wife, my children, my life with a passion I had misplaced some years before. Not all of this is credited to our father-son meeting, but it certainly was a major catalyst during that time.

I have thanked my dad in many ways since that confrontation; this essay is my latest, but not my last, gift of appreciation and honoring. Perhaps the greatest gift that I have given and received, however, was the christening of a new relationship on that day, the day I began to call my dad ... my friend.

5

WHOSE EYES

(Scribner)

♦

"Who does he look like?" An asinine question. He looks like himself. Precisely. Not like you. Not like me. Not like grandma, grandpa, or cousin Joe. He looks exactly like himself. If you squeeze him into pre-formed categories, he might spend the rest of his days trying to squirm out of them, as a butterfly from an ill-fitting, second-hand cocoon. There's no need to focus on how he's like someone else; focusing on how he's unique will do just fine.

And that strong, sturdy chin you say he got from grandpa? How sturdy will it be for *him*, if it's merely borrowed? Can strength be built upon something that is not one's own? And he has his father's nose, does he? Then let's return that nose to its rightful owner – he might need it at the finish line of a close race someday. And whose eyes does he have? His mother's? This must adversely affect her vision; how will she ever see *him* clearly?

So, he's toilet-trained later than his sister was? But reading earlier? And more verbal? But less outgoing? Little good can come of conveying any of this to children. Kids don't want to be compared to anyone or anything; they want to be loved and acknowledged for who they are – not who they aren't, not who we need them to be. The child who's preoccupied with sifting through "how he's like whom" will never get around to looking at who he *is*.

Parenting, done right, is like being a rapt spectator at the theater, captivated by the story unfolding on the stage before you. You know the basic story line; you know the key elements that will be present, and the general sequence in which they'll unfold. The wonder is in seeing the nuances and spins *this* person puts on the role. The focus is on how he makes the stock role his own; how he brings it to life in a new way.

Kids are like this too; they all follow the same developmental path; the excitement is in seeing how they each navigate their way, and what unique detours they take along the way. Too many parents chart out the course and then waste most of their precious parenting energy trying to ensure that the child travels in a straight line on *this* path, moving steadily onward as they hear the whip crack behind them, avoiding the potentially enriching but inefficient detours. Kids instinctively resist this.

In parenting, there's really not all that much to *do* – keep the kids away from danger for the first few years; teach them about the wonders and hazards of living (making sure to strike a balance between the two), feed them from time to time, and teach them, by example, how to love and be loved. The rest they'll take care of by themselves. Trust them. It's wired in. They'll find their way.

Once you're steadily doing these things, the parenting fun begins. You get to sit back and watch. See what unfolds; focus on getting to know who they are, rather than concerning yourself with making them into a particular sort of person. See what ways they'll find to surprise you. See how their actions will create both the opportunity and the need for *you* to continue growing, to get up off that cushion of self-restricting familiarity you've been sitting on for a few decades, and stretch a bit. See what they can teach you about life that you used to know but have forgotten. Kids are great refreshers for adults. Their gaze penetrates where adult perception merely glances off the surface. They know what really matters. Their perspective on life is wonderfully uncomplicated.

Children expand as they mature. It happens all by itself. They blossom. They open up, becoming more three-dimensional, like a wad of plastic wrap that was crumpled and then released. You don't have to tug at them. You don't have to *make* them expand; it's a perfectly natural process.

Kids are born crumpled, and they spend their life un-crumpling, little by little. At the moment of birth, their faces are always smushed and wrinkled. At three months of age, their legs are still crumpled; they pop into the air when you lay the baby on its back. A bit later language unfolds; the sounds were in there all along, but they have to jumble around for a while before they get into the right arrangement. During the school years, independent judgment appears as damp, limp wings which gradually dry and strengthen if they're allowed to remain spread. By the teen years, it's the child's humility and perspective that are restricted and in need of expansion. But even then, you don't have to tug at them to get them to expand; just give it some time, and watch with wonder as it happens. It will happen. You just need to be patient. And bear witness. And, most of all, stay out of the way.

6

WORKING, PLAYING

(Scribner)

♦

Y ou're going to forget what I'm about to tell you. If you're at all like me, that is. I *try* to remember, but I still can't make it stick. As a father, though, I have an easily-accessible reminder – If only I would pay more attention to it.

The reminder is: children.

The lesson is: "work" and "play" are NOT OPPOSITES.

I'm going against the tide of 35 years' worth of learning here, so I'll repeat it for my own benefit: *work and play are not opposites.* They're states of mind, attitudes, styles of approaching an activity. And they're not incompatible with each other. In fact, they blend very nicely.

One crisp autumn day, I went out to clear the backyard of the sweet-gum tree balls that had been littering it for several weeks. Abby was bored, and wanted me to play with her. I suggested that she come help me with the yard-work (yeah, right, Dad. Nice try). She grumbled something about it not being fun, and off-the-cuff I said "Okay, how about doing some yard-*play* then?"

She looked at me thoughtfully before drifting off to the far corner of the yard. I began raking up the prickly balls. I had almost filled the first brown yard-waste bag before I realized that I hadn't heard a word from Abby. Looking up, I saw her approaching me with her cupped hands outstretched, carrying an offering of a dozen or so sweet-gum balls.

Then she spoke, in the dreamy, sing-song voice she uses when she's deeply involved in fantasy play. "Father, here you are – I made breakfast for you. I know you must be hungry after working for so long on our farm. Here, take your food and I'll go and feed the animals, too."

With a bit of inquiry, I soon deduced that we were a farm family, and the farmer's daughter had the chores of preparing breakfast, feeding the livestock, milking the cows, and gathering the eggs from the hen-house.

Loosening my own perspective, I let my imagination spin off to where I could join her. My yard-waste bag became, surrealistically, the centralized stomach for the entire farm, and all food intended for either the family members or the animals was to be put into it. She retrieved an old bucket from the garage to capture slightly lumpy-looking "milk" from the cows, and we decided it was best to "drink" it right away (... into the "stomach" it goes!). Her repeated trips to the hen-house (which evidently housed some very prolific chickens) yielded a plethora of bristly, round ... you get the idea.

Before long, we had the yard cleared. In my work, I played a bit. As Abby played, she worked a bit. I know that my work was enriched and lightened once I let some playfulness into it. The time passed quickly. My curiosity about what Abby might do next kept my mind off of the futility of trying to keep up with the mess made by those accursed trees. And it seemed that Abby's play was enriched by knowing that she was providing a "service" as well as using her imagination. Between the two of us, the line distinguishing "work" from "play" got pretty thin.

Adults often approach the activities that fill their day as "jobs," and view them as drudgery because of this. To a child, every activity holds the possibility of play. I vaguely recall knowing this when I was young. Somewhere along the way, somewhere in my years and years of schooling, perhaps, that knowledge got crowded out by other things.

It's coming back to me, though. I've come to realize how important that knowledge is. Now I just wish I could remember it.

7

PICKING UP BABY

(Scribner)

♦

Having gathered my little one into my arms, I raise my leg gingerly over the baby-blocker gate, the dam which separates the infants from the toddlers at the day-care center. As I step across, a crowd of toddlers materializes and flows toward us. With their faces tilted upward, they resemble a field of sunflowers, turning to follow me and the son. Slowly, steadily, I wade through the field, which now begins to sway.

It's properly called toddling, I suppose. But when a roomful begins to move *en masse*, the effect is surreal. The feet shuffle purposefully but unsteadily; the arms do not move; the trunk does, but with a Parkinsonian sway. The hungry, longing eyes together with the ungraceful, somnambulistic movement of the bodies calls to mind a scene from "Night of the Living Dead" shrunk to one-quarter scale. They stare, intensely curious yet unspeaking. Each face consists of three orbs: two, wide and questioning, astride the nose; the third beneath it, silently pumping to the sucking rhythm.

Slowly reaching out to us, they grasp at us. Two damp sticky hands clutch my trouser leg; a third stretches to reach my belt; a teething mouth locks onto the tassel of my shoe. My son jerks his leg up in surprise, wresting his foot from the jaws of the Great White Toddler below. The toddlers nudge one another, Pee-Wee hockey players wobbly on their feet and wearing well-cushioned pants, their Pamper-padded collisions intended to gain the advantage of better position. One goes down, landing squarely on his rump. He rises and rejoins the fracas; no acknowledgment of the fall shows on his face.

For a moment I am Jesus carrying the cross up Calvary, and they clutter the path, boisterously, relentlessly clamoring either to touch my raiment or to stone me. Then I realize it is not me they want, but what I bear. They are looking at my son, not me. Their trouser-grabbing is not an end in itself, but a means to climb up to the exalted position my son has.

I'm suddenly aware of how *tall* I am. I stand a shade over six feet now, but throughout my childhood I was small, usually the smallest in my class at school. Even after the high-school growth spurt (seven inches in a year) which flung me to the other side of the growth-chart's midpoint, I retained the inward sense of myself as "small."

But tip-toeing amidst the children at my feet, I'm struck by the undeniable fact that I'm "big" from the vantage point of a child. That means that

I'm "big" in my son's eyes as well. As he matures, his view of me as "big" will transform in meaning -- he'll unquestioningly view me as wise, as having answers, as trustworthy, as reliable, as strong ...

I now feel "big," in a way I never did before becoming a father. It's like an *inward* growth spurt has occurred, and I'm surprised that the responsibility of being all the things just mentioned does not intimidate me. That responsibility is something I can embrace, even cradle in my arms, holding it with cautiousness, care ... and confidence.

8

FOLLOW-UP THERE

(Scribner)

♦

My own projections ran rampant. I tagged my son, then all of nine months old, as the impetus for my own continued development as an individual. At that age, he appeared to me unrestrained, carefree, too joyful to be cautious. I steeled my nerves for the personal stretches I would have to make to keep pace with him.

Now, not quite three years later, he's turning into a half-scale clone of me. Timid. Slow to warm up to people. Clingy in novel situations. Risk-averse. So much for my stretching. My new challenge is to find ways to honor and value the qualities in him that I often despise in myself.

I think I'd prefer the *other* challenge. This one is far more difficult.

When *I* approach new relationships, or consider some significant life change, I'm usually seized first by fear, and feel myself wanting to turn away from whatever it is that is threatening to me. Daniel is three, and when *he* feels that way, he literally does what I feel like doing. He turns away, hides behind my legs, pulls me toward the exit.

His mother and I figured that he'd meet this challenge best in a context where he felt capable and comfortable. Daniel is agile and well-coordinated. At age three, he somersaults every bit as gracefully as his sister who is twice his age.

The solution? A six-session pre-schooler gymnastics class. Nice thick mats to tumble on. Trained spotters for the genuine balance beam, which would afford challenges beyond the railroad-tie walking he's already mastered. Warm, engaging instructors who understand and enjoy children.

My wife made the arrangements for the class, and we agreed that I would be the one to take him. "He's less clingy with you, and has an easier time separating from you than from me," Susan said to me. She was right. But that's not why I agreed – even insisted – on being the one to take him.

I needed to take him in order to wrestle my way through my intolerance of timidity, fearfulness, and shying away from new situations. You'll note that I'm not specifying *whose* timidity and fearfulness I'm referring to. That's intentional on my part, because wrestling with *his* timidity and fearfulness is also an effort to come to terms with my own.

I need to do that; I've been noticing lately how I pull away from Daniel a bit when he's behaving in those ways. It gets in the way of my ability to prize him, to be close to him. With further scrutiny of what is going in within myself around this stuff, I eventually recognize that the path through this is to keep my own fear and timidity squarely before me, and to use it to help me step inside Daniel's world at those moments when he's feeling timid and scared. And then to respond to *his* fears in a more sensitive, understanding way than I respond to my own.

In the first class, my mantra is "whatever he does or doesn't do is exactly right for him; accept and tolerate it." I struggle through the class. The instructors are warm and inviting, yet Daniel repeatedly buries his head in my lap. I embrace him, but simultaneously feel my legs and pelvis stiffen, as if I would rather buck him off my lap. I exhale more loudly that I'd intended to. My face feels flushed. I notice I'm avoiding eye contact with the instructors, as I try to conceal my shame and discomfort at what's transpiring. I – we – barely make it through the class.

The following Saturday is much the same, except this time Daniel sits down *behind* me, peeking around my torso just long enough to say "no" to the instructors trying to entice him onto the mat. Mentally, I'm barely there with him; I'm spinning into my own recollections, memories both remote and recent, of feeling pushed to do something I feared, of being expected (by myself or others) to do something I wasn't ready for, and my failure to stand my ground and say "no."

With that awareness, I felt a shift. Daniel is *not* just like me. He's different; he *is* saying "no." Dad's usual manner of resolving these dilemmas has often been to yield, to go along with it, only halfheartedly participating, and secretly resenting being "pushed" into it. That's my ugly truth.

But my little boy is claiming a kind of strength, showing a kind of determination in the midst of his fearfulness. He knows what he's ready for and what he's not ready for, and his actions square with that bit of self-awareness.

As I recognize this, my struggle ceases. I am able to prize his self-awareness and his willingness to let it steer his actions. Hell, he's better at it than I am.

Maybe I *will* learn from him, and maybe he *will* inspire me to continue to stretch in my individual development. I'll have to, if I'm to be the father he deserves.

The other result of all this is that it became clear to me that there was no need to continue with gymnastics class right now. And while I hate to admit it, it seems that it was "time to stop" only after *I* had gleaned that new piece of awareness.

Now Daniel and I play together at home during that Saturday morning time. It's good. The gymnastics experience also inspired a poem, which I've titled "Beautiful, Dutiful Children":

When preschool children take gymnastics classes,
They're frightened, so they cling and whine and fuss.
We patiently affirm we're there for them;
*They wipe their tears and stay – they're there for **us**.*

We're learning.

LESSONS IN LIFE

One father is more than a hundred schoolmasters.

-- English Proverb

9

FAITH

(Frey)

♦

My son gave me a lesson in life, again, recently. It's several weeks before Christmas, and Nathan approaches me and speaks in his, "I just discovered another great truth" voice:

"Dad, there's no Santa Claus" (he's 4, no, 4¾ years old at the time of this deduction).

"Oh? How did you decide that?"

"Well, the guys at the mall aren't the real Santa. I've never seen or touched the real Santa. I don't believe in things I can't touch or see."

"Huh (a snappy response for all dads who need to buy some time). Soooo (Time Buying: The Sequel), have you ever seen or touched God?"

"No."

"Do you believe in God?"

"Sure ... sometimes."

"OK."

Two weeks later: It's Christmas Eve and Nathan puts treats on the fireplace hearth for Santa, along with carrots for the reindeer, of course.

By his actions, Nathan reminds me that faith is about believing in what I cannot prove, sometimes cannot see or touch. Magic, real magic, is what may occur because of faith.

He also teaches me that faith is imperfect, as am I, and there is no shame in that. The absolute believer who suffers no crises of faith is often the fanatic who will kill another human's spirit in the name of righteousness, a truly frightening creature. Those of us who are both full of faith, the faithful, and full of honesty are believers ... sometimes. *True believers have doubt AND hope ... true skeptics held, lost, and need to reclaim faith.*

10

THE BIRDS AND THE BEES

(Frey)

♦

My sister Lisa claims she taught me about sex. I have no memory of this. I do recall mom giving me a little pink book to read, something like, "All About Boys and Girls"; telling me that I could ask her any question I generated from the pages. Yeah, sure ... "Hey, mom, what really turns girls on?" "Well, son, you'll have to find out in your next lifetime, because you're terminally grounded and will have to care for me after the heart-attack I'm getting ready to have." Oddly, I wasn't sure what I didn't know about sex but I was absolutely confident that the questions of most interest to me were not material for a June and Beav conversation around the kitchen table with mom.

And so, I am eternally grateful to two girls, who shall go unnamed, one of whom gave me a more useful book to read that taught me a modicum of sexual proficiency, thus saving me from any more than one boatload and several decades of misinformation and embarrassment; the other who gave me my first practical experience and the benefit of her superior skill. Unfortunately, as with many of the men I know, that loving information was blended with the shame-based sexual teachings of the 50's, the "if it feels good do it" propaganda of casual sex in the 60's and 70's, the onslaught of pornography in the 80's, and the sex-can-now-be-deadly reality of the 90's.

How then, as a father, am I prepared to lovingly teach my children about healthy sex and intimacy in this world of mixed messages, in a culture which both idealizes and demonizes sex? As a U.S. citizen, I am familiar with no other culture that spends more time, money, and energy selling sex as separate from relationship and intimacy, at the same time continuing to sell moralistic fear and shame. Sex ain't rocket science; how did this all get so complicated? What to do?

I can only tell you what *I* did. I found other men and women who were facing, and openly discussing, this struggle. And in these connections with other parents who have bridged this wide and treacherous river I began to see four commonalties that I hope you will find useful. First, we went out and re-armed ourselves with quality information, information we missed in our early development. Personally, I have reviewed materials for children from pre-school to high-school, along with adult information on the romantic, erotic, gender, communication and spiritual aspects of sex. Second, we have listened to and learned from our loving partners about passion and pleasure ...

commitment and unconditional love. When DiAnne and I model love, affection, and respect, we provide a picture of sexuality that is contained within a vital, committed relationship. I cannot count the number of confused folks I have met with over the years who have no memory of their parents touching each other in loving ways; a hug, a good-bye kiss; some of whom heard sexual innuendo, but saw no affection. Giving our children information is not enough, they need to *see* what intimacy in action looks like. Third, many of us have faced, with help, our struggles with sexual confusion, misinformation, shame, and compulsion. This often involves releasing and reworking past sexual trauma; healing the pain of the sexual wounds we have suffered and often, in our ignorance, visited upon others. Finally, we have learned to talk with our children about what we have learned. This is no small task. When do we talk? How much information do I give them at what age? How do I deal with their discomfort ... and my own? What if they ask questions that I don't have answers for? What if one of my children is more knowledgeable, or more sexually active than I believe he or she is ready for? Or than *I* am ready for? These are big questions. I can tell you what I do; I return to those same men and women and keep discussing my questions, my concerns, my joy, my fear. Then, I make a plan and act on it.

Those of you who are reading this essay may need all four steps, or you may only need one or two. If you are a man with children, I suspect you need something. This is a brave new world, and sex is no longer only about procreation, or morality, or pleasure; it's about all of these *and* knowledge and responsibility and love and safety. In today's world sex is life and, for some, death. For my children, to the extent of my power, I chose life and pleasure and love and safety. Beyond providing them with technical data and a moral code, I endeavor to understand who they are and what they need in the context of the world they live in today. Fathers who will teach well are committed students.

11

JUST BEES

(Scribner)

♦

I was reading a newspaper article about bees, their benefits in nature, and the myths about how dangerous they are to humans. The large cartoon drawing of a bee which accompanied the article caught Abby's interest, and she asked what the story was about. I proceeded to summarize the article for her. I read the excerpt that said that bee stings hurt the bee more than they hurt humans, since for the bee, a sting means death.

"I knew that," said Abby. "Bees can only sting once, because when they do it, they die."

I was about to continue with the excerpt, which explained that when the barbed stinger penetrates skin, and the bee flies away, some of the bee's anatomy remains attached to the stinger, which eventuates in the bee's death. But before I could continue, Abby began elaborating on her own understanding about the matter.

"The reason it dies is because when a bee stings you, it puts ALL of its energy into the sting, and so it doesn't have any energy left for its own life, so it dies. But some bees don't sting much – like bumblebees. They *know* that stinging a person means that they'll have to die, and bumblebees are much smarter than the other kinds of bees, so they don't sting people much. They're just a lot smarter. That's why they're bigger than other bees; it's because their brains are so much bigger, and they have to have enough room for their big brains."

I accepted her version, and saw no need to augment it with the remainder of what was said in the article. I was fascinated by her thought process. Looking at her, I could almost see the wheels turning in her head, as she sought to make connections among the various facts she has absorbed, and to weave them together into a coherent understanding.

Often, it is father's role to introduce his children to the world at large, to expose them to facts, principles, and information about the world that we hold to be objective Truths. Part of that process involves correcting misconceptions. But in this instance, it occurred to me that the more important thing that was happening was that Abby was using her own style of thinking to arrive at an understanding which, if not certifiably "true" by scientific standards, at least satisfied her need to make sense of the world.

It's easy for children to grow up believing that they must look *outward* (to the world, to reference books, to other people) to discern what is "true." And of course, in certain circumstances, it's important to do just that. But there's a danger there: that the child will come to believe that the quest for "truth" can *only* be satisfied by looking outward. And adult life certainly reinforces that perception; there's no shortage of "experts" who are willing to be cited on most topics.

What's neglected in this process is the child's confidence in and valuation of his or her own inner sense of what's true, right, just. Without that, children are left to operate from an ever-shifting foundation of whatever the current surroundings (or latest experts) tell them. The person who looks outward for Truth is limited to either accepting that external truth, or reacting against it. The vital alternative of reaching within to grasp for an individual, possibly new and creative truth, is lost. Yet when greatness bursts upon the scene, it's often the result of the person coming up with a novel view or understanding, a genuinely creative solution. The world would benefit from more of that.

My daughter is bright. The day will come when she will grasp the science of insect anatomy. But I'm not going to rush her to get there. I'd rather see where her concept of "large bodies housing large brains" leads her. I'm curious, too, to see what comes of her views on what occurs when one puts *all* of one's energy into something. Perhaps you die. But perhaps you achieve something wonderful.

12

PACIFISTS WITH GUNS

(Frey)

◆

I am anti-war down the line, to the core. Never fired a gun at man, woman, child nor beast. No BB guns, toy Winchesters or ray guns in our house. I believe that if the NRA bought food instead of lobbyists, we'd be able to feed most of the hungry humans on the planet, and any remaining funds could subsidize therapy services for militia members. I've spent countless hours in the psychotherapy trenches helping families stop and heal the effects of domestic violence. Most of the gun play I'm familiar with is about desperate people engaged in desperate acts.

So, when Nathan came home from a visit to a family friend last week with a squirt gun, I was faced with a sizable dilemma. You see, I really like squirt guns; I mean, *really* like them. I like to fill them up when no one's looking, sneak up on my wife or kids in the yard on a hot summer's day, and Zap ... Pow ... Splash! AND worse yet, this was no ordinary squirter, not one of those puny see-through green or pink pistols with the water capacity of a tea cup and the range of a good spit. No, this was the pump-action stupendo soaker with a reservoir the size of Lake Erie. And so, looking this predicament straight in the eye, I stepped up and made exactly the kind of tough decision that fathers around the world must often make: "We're going out tomorrow and we're going to buy another squirt gun ... for me ... and no weenie one, either; I'm going for the big soaker." Nathan gazed upon me with joy, anticipation and an absolute understanding of the walking, talking incongruity that stood before him. You see, we'd discussed this issue before:

Nate: "Dad, how come I can't have guns and you don't like guns, but I can have squirt guns?" The kid cuts right to the heart of the matter ... I wonder where he learned that?

Me: "Uh ... uh ... uh ... weeeelllll ... "

As I stall, I realize that almost anything I say will be inconsistent and quite possibly dishonest. I opt for inconsistent and honest.

"Well ... I really like squirt guns."

"OK."

OK ... OK ... What a kid!

The next morning, as planned, we ventured out and returned to home base with a mega-squirter, and immediately put it to the test of sun and fun.

Now you may be wondering how I intend to clear up the double message I've been sending my son. I'm working on that, although he already seems pretty clear about the difference between real play and real violence. We have talked about toys vs.

weapons and I know that over time my wise and wily son will grasp the implications of ... Anyway, gotta go. DiAnne is in the garden and the kids are playing in the yard and it's a hot day, and ....

13

BICYCLING

(Scribner)

♦

This story is a boastful one. I've always thought of myself as a teacher, and today I had it confirmed that I am one, and a good one at that. The evaluation came from the student, and was corroborated by the objective outcome of what was taught. Today, I taught Abby to ride a two-wheeler.

I've been thinking it through since we got back home, and I've boiled the lesson down to the essence of fatherly teaching.

1) I assessed and confirmed her readiness to move ahead.

2) I broke the task down into its component parts for her, planning out the sequence of steps to be mastered, and kept in mind the order in which they should be tackled.

3) I set up moderate challenges for her, while

4) being mindful of her personal safety and

5) her self-esteem (#s 4 and 5 were monitored constantly throughout the lesson).

6) I relied on recollections of my own past experience with new learning to empathize with her current experience.

7) I praised effort rather than outcome.

8) I shared, REALLY shared, in her joy when she began to "get it."

9) I recorded the event for posterity – three times (once in my memory, once in my camera, once in this essay).

This aspect of fathering is a bit different from the simple "unconditional positive regard" that is so widely touted. Were I to limit myself to that, my daughter's learning curve would have been much longer, and her scrapes and bruises more numerous. No, there are times when the father/teacher's role is to point out errors and risks, to offer honest yet fair criticism, to push or challenge, to point out unpleasant truths -- but of course to do it all in a loving, supportive way. I do allow her to struggle to find her own way through things; but occasionally, she's travelling such a dead end road that I feel the only caring thing to do is intervene. This is especially true in physical tasks; certain mechanical aspects of riding a bike (or swimming, or swinging a baseball bat) really can make the difference between success and failure.

She concluded the lesson by saying "I can really ride a bike, and I can ride it really well! All it really takes is lots of practice! Next we'll have to tackle roller skating!"

14

SKATING

(Scribner)

♦

She had never roller skated before. She was among friends who were, for the most part, more accomplished skaters. Abby does not like being the one who can't do something. She is determined, persistent, strong-willed, and perfectionistic. She is impatient with her shortcomings, and seeks to overcome them through sheer will-power. She has countless gifts and talents, but coordination and grace are not high on that list. Her moods are intense and mercurial, but she does have days when she is, in her words, "as happy as bubble gum." She is caring and empathic; she is responsive to life's music; she has the perceptiveness, imagination, and vocabulary of a poet. But she is also gangly, has big feet, and tenses up when she's nervous. The fluid motion of skating doesn't come naturally to her.

Even as a competent athlete, I can recall and empathize with the crush of humiliation that accompanies a poor performance in front of others. It's a feeling of disappearing; of shrinking down smaller and smaller, becoming a dense, burning, blushing mass of matter with some tremendous atomic weight. If I had that experience more than once in a given sport, I'd usually resolve not to play that sport any more.

Abby reacts differently. When she realizes she's failing (and it's obvious she does realize this), she responds by redoubling her efforts. The hard part is that once she's already upset, her efforts become increasingly disorganized and decreasingly effective. She cries, pounds the floor, and lashes out at anyone who tries to lend a hand.

On this, her first day roller skating, her repeated response to my efforts at helping is "*No*, Deeda; you go skate *far* away from me!" She didn't want my help. She didn't want me to witness her struggle, either.

Unable to persuade her to accept help, I ended up skating by myself, "far away." I felt guilty doing so. I'm a decent roller-skater, and I enjoyed gliding around the rink, weaving in and out among the small people. Whenever I could, I'd sneak a glance at her as she struggled to make it around the rink. I was seized by the idea that I might be humiliating her all the more by zipping around effortlessly, without falling. I worried that the guards and the other parents there would think I was being neglectful or cruel, leaving my struggling daughter to fend for herself.

I was in a bind – the discrepancy between *my* need to be helpful and *her* need to be independent was so vast that I couldn't see a good solution. I have occasionally resolved such situations by bowing to the pressure I feel from the glares of the other adults, and using my "strength and authority" as a father to reprimand her or somehow intimidate her into stopping her display. As my *inward* strength and conviction as a father grows, however, I do that less and less. In my more lucid moments, I *know* that doing what makes *me* (and perhaps the other parents) more comfortable is often at odds with what's in my daughter's best interests. At those moments, I recognize clearly and vividly that my duty – as a dues-paying member of the noble profession of parenthood – is to give priority to what my daughter needs emotionally, not to what will make the grown-ups comfortable.

Maybe she is a person who just needs to struggle and find her own way through things. I really did try to help her out; her response, loud and clear, was "that is not what I need from you." She has demonstrated in other situations that she's able to tell me what she needs from me. It stands to reason that she probably knows just as well what she *doesn't* need. As a parent, I do want to encourage her to make and act on those distinctions.

My fathering challenge in all this was to accept that placing her needs above mine can be uncomfortable for me, just as Abby's pursuit of autonomy is uncomfortable for her at times. But these are the necessary discomforts that are part and parcel of growth. So, my job was to breathe, tolerate my own uneasiness with the process, and accept that what was happening was exactly what needed to be happening.

In the car on the way home we were silent for awhile. I felt like I should try to praise her, give her some "positive strokes" for her efforts, but I worried that it would come across as forced, artificial, too far removed from what her experience of the afternoon had been. As I struggled over what to say, my ever-loving daughter bailed me out.

"Deeda ... um ... well ... at least I only fell down *twice* that last time around."

I smiled and took advantage of the opening she'd provided. "Only *TWICE?!* That's only *one* more time than Tara Lipinski fell in that competition we saw on t.v. last night!" She cocked her head thoughtfully, then gave a single giggle.

Small-talk reigned for the remainder of the ride home. I pulled into the garage; we got out of the car, then wordlessly walked hand-in-hand through the kitchen door. I reached into my pocket, took out a piece of bubble gum for myself, and offered her a piece. She accepted.

15

DANGER ... WARNING

(Frey)

♦

Wjhat might be a father's worse fear for his child? That she'll poke her eye out with a stick? Or fall from a tree and break her neck? Or contract a dread disease? Or fart in church? No, my informal research suggests a much larger, more personal paternal nightmare ... the sheer terror that my child will make the same mistakes in life that I have!

This hypothesis simmered in my gray matter as I motored through the countryside with my 16 year old, Carly, tonight. In the midst of our discussion about Carly's life, the nasal tone of Country Joe McDonald emerges from the dashboard radio. You middle-agers and retro-rockers know who I mean: the lead singer of Country Joe and The Fish, Woodstock survivor and performer of *The Fixin' to Die Rag*, *The Fish Cheer* ("Give me an F ... U ... C ..." etc.). Joe is hosting a retrospective on KSHE, Real Rock Radio, on the Psychedelic

Era. The parallel is not lost on me – country*side*; Country *Joe* ... and my mind begins to wander back to a mood-altered drive through rural Iowa, another country night, some 20 years ago; one of moving mailboxes, singing trees and highway lines turning to snakes before my dilated pupils. No, the symbolism of the Psychedelic Era and tonight's drive are not lost on me.

Sinking deeper into my road trance meanderings, I imagine ...

Joe McDonald is sitting in his living-room. The walls are filled with cool photos of him hanging out with Janis, Jimi, Jerry, Grace and the gang. Joe's a survivor, perhaps a worker and a family man. In through the front door bounds Joe, Jr., complete with a tie-dyed T-shirt (90's style) and a Pearl Jam lunch box. Little Joe is looking a bit sheepish.

"Problem at school, son?"

"Well, I got detention today, dad."

"What happened, pal? Civil disobedience?"

"Not exactly. It was my turn to talk about what my father did for a living and all I did was sing that cool song I heard on your Woodstock CD; you know, *The Fish Cheer*. The teacher got real irritated."

"Well, you see son, that song's based on a word that doesn't go over real big in school."

"C'mon, dad, you sang it in front of 500,000 people."

"Welll ... That was *different*, son. It was the 60's; we were speaking out against a horrific war; the song was a metaphor for our anti-establish- ... Oh, never mind, just do your time and don't say the F-word in school anymore."

"Whatever."

You see, it's common knowledge in parenting circles that modeling healthy behavior is the key to the parenting process; my kids will do as I do with much greater consistency than they will do as I say. But, what about what I already did? Perhaps some of you have no stories of misspent youth; if so you're in the clear on this issue, probably had an extremely healthy and perhaps boring childhood and can simply jump ahead to the next story. Many of us, myself included, are not so fortunate. Oh sure, I could hope my kids don't ask about my past – but it's too late. My teenagers already have. I could tell them only carefully selected instances of my mature, well-mannered behavior; for most of my early years I *was* well-mannered. I could fall back on the time-tested, usually futile refrain of "I hope you learn from my mistakes and don't have to make them yourself."

I know – let's return to Country Joe in hope that the fairy tale has some wisdom to offer. I'm guessing Joe decides to come clean with his kid, first seeking the wise counsel of those he trusts, taking time to determine how much information to disclose to his child at this stage of his life. He will commit to answering his child's questions to the best of his ability. He'll use his past as a teaching story; a parable of survival, redemption, renewal. He will talk about the best parts of those times, and there were many; he will honestly speak of the worst. He will neither condone nor romanticize his past choices; he will speak of the risks and the costs, to himself and others. Then, Joe will vow to love, support and guide his child through the choppy waters of his own journey toward adulthood. That's what Joe will do. Anyway, that's **my** guess; that's **my** plan.

16

SWIMMING

(Scribner)

♦

W hen Abby decided it was time to master the water, Susan and I arranged for a two-fronted attack: on one hand, formal swim lessons; on the other, ongoing support, encouragement, and informal assistance from us. At the pool one day, Abby was unusually upset about her efforts to learn to tread water. I offered to go in with her and help her out in whatever way she needed, but she seemed too frightened even for that. Finally, she agreed to enter the water, but refused to go into the water over her head unless I'd hold onto her the entire time. I agreed to do so, talking with her all the while, trying to calm her, and trying to understand her fear.

She clung to me, occasionally scratching my bare back. I was aware of two very different ways to deal with her. The first, the "instinctive" one that I'm usually least proud of, was to dismiss her fears, and push her to somehow "just get over it." But as I stayed with her, seeking to "push" instead through my own resistance, my second option became clear. I felt honored by the trust she was putting in me, asking me to support her, emotionally and physically. I admired her ability to recognize her fears and limits and to express her needs, and I saw an opportunity to help her learn to traverse that fine line between respecting one's fear and pushing to stretch one's limits.

By listening carefully to the exact nature of her fear, I learned that it was about "not having control." It wasn't so much a fear of deep water; it was fear that if the swimming instructor said "we have to practice this at the deep end," Abby couldn't decline or try it first in shallower water. It was the fear that the final decision would not be hers to make.

Together, we came up with a more tolerable way for her to practice. I focused on giving her more control. I showed her that as she was treading water and beginning to tire, she could take a deep breath, allow herself to sink down, touch bottom (in five feet of water), and push off the bottom to regain her "altitude." She took to this idea like ... well ... like the proverbial duck to water, and practiced it over and over, smiling each time she surfaced, clearly pleased with herself. She would bounce up and down, sinking and rising, until she grew tired (or perhaps bored) with it, and then paddle over to the side by herself. After pausing to catch her breath, she'd swim the eight feet or so back to me, "docking" on me only briefly to steady herself before she resumed her intentional treading-sinking-and-rising exercise.

This felt like a very fatherly role to me: to offer a sturdy, safe haven within which the child feels secure, while simultaneously offering encouragement and guidance as to how to take some risks. It's been said that people "plunge ahead" into difficult tasks when they realize they simply *must* – the old "sink or swim" theory. But I learned from my daughter that sometimes it works just as well to convey the message that whether or not you "plunge ahead," the support is there, and it's okay to plunge ahead on your own terms, if and when you feel ready to do so.

I often have difficulty adopting that attitude toward my own fears and insecurities. That's an area of ongoing work for me, but I *am* finding that as I gradually get better at it, I also find myself much more patient with the fears that my children express. It has become very clear to me that the extent to which I'm able to tolerate and accept *their* fears mirrors the extent to which I can tolerate my own.

17

POVERTY

(Frey)

♦

I have been without money.

I have never been without prospects.

In 1980 I arrived in Sterling, Ill. with my brand spanking new Masters degree, my pregnant spouse, a new job, all the bills paid up for one month ... and $12 in the bank. This was a step up, from an efficiency apartment, a graduate assistantship, and no money in the bank. My wife and I had known, for most of our time together, what it was like to live week to week, month to month. I also knew I was educated, had the backing of my family and hers if we got in a desperate jam, and I possessed a work ethic that just never quit. So, as I awaited the birth of my first child I did not live in the fears that some parents I have met deal with every day: Will I be able to feed my child enough to quell the hunger pains today? Will the heat be turned off? Should I buy *food* or *medicine* for my child? How will I go to work with no one but me to care for my baby?

I'm certain there are political answers to these questions. I have sat in the company of many self-proclaimed experts over the years; most of them were people like me, folks who have been without money, but not without prospects. Today, I wonder how I would have coped without a belief in my potential to improve my situation?

Due to the efforts of my parents, who grew up in the Depression and knew poverty, I have never had a hungry day, a winter without a warm coat, a dark night with no electricity. We didn't have a whole lot of money, but what we did have was hope and I was taught to believe that I had an exciting and successful future ahead of me. I was provided all the necessities, plus, with a bit of hard work on my part, 19 years of education. I had prospects.

As a father, I have offered my children the same passionate belief about a hopeful future. Not the pie-in-the-sky propaganda I have heard so often from the "just pull yourself up by your bootstraps" folks. Rather, I offer the lessons I've learned: one part innate ability + one part hard work + one part belief in a great Creator + one part the loving efforts of those around you = success on levels not imagined on any financial statement. In doing so, I find that I have two teenagers in the house, neither of whom has any clear picture of their future, who do believe they have prospects. Each speaks of continuing her education beyond high school as simply a natural process. They speak in general terms of careers that are financially stable, emotionally satisfying, and that give worth to our planet. I believe they will find these paths.

I often wonder about the children who see no prospects. I visit with them every day. Some are clients and I attempt to loan them a sense of vision and passion to move beyond the places they are stuck, emotionally, financially, spiritually. Some pass through my life as service workers in motels, the places where I eat, buy goods, travel to and from. For them, I find myself wishing for some magic touch, a blessing to put sparkle in their eyes, to rekindle desire in their hearts, to create focus in their minds.

Naïve? Sure. Those with prospects can afford to dream.

I was listening to Carly as she spoke the other day about prospects; her dreams for educational and career and material success. And as my listening came to a close, I launched into Dad Lecture 101 on the merits of sharing your success with those who have less. Carly, in a voice frighteningly like her father's, stopped me and said, "I'd guess after living with you and DiAnne all these years I probably already know that, dad. I'll help other people, too."

Those with prospects can make a difference. Carly already knows that.

TRANSITIONS

Even a minor event in the life of a child is an event of that child's world and thus a world event.

-- Gaston Bachelard

18

PAINT

(Scribner)

♦

This morning, around 8:30, I heard muffled sounds coming from Abby's room. I went up to check on her, and found her sitting in the middle of the floor, sobbing. I sat down next to her, wiped a few big tears from her cheeks, and asked what the trouble was. She looked at me, hesitating, uncertain whether to disclose the source of her upset.

"Deeda, I don't know how to say this ... There's something I feel I *need* to tell you, but I'm really worried that it's gonna hurt your feelings."

We briefly weighed her dilemma, and eventually decided that maybe it would be best for her to tell me what was going on. I told her I was willing to hear about it, since it was obviously something pretty important to her.

Still wary, she began. "Deeda, I don't know how to tell you this, but I was looking around my room, at those bears on the border that goes around the walls, and it looks kind of like they're all wearing diapers, and whenever I look at them it makes me feel like I'm a baby."

I looked around at her walls. She had a valid point. Here she was, a month shy of her seventh birthday, and her room is still festooned with little pink-and-blue bears with toddler-like proportions. Distinctly cute, but distinctly un-cool for a rising second-grader.

"I see what you mean. And you were worried that I'd be upset about that, huh?"

"Well, it's just that I know how hard you worked to put those bears up on the wall when I was a little kid."

Re-doing her bedroom was the first internal improvement I had attempted as a new homeowner. I vividly recalled the solid day's work of stripping the old wallpaper, scraping, prepping, painting the walls *and* the inside of the closet (in her chosen shade of pink), doing the trim in white, and topping it all off with the adhesive border printed with alternating teddy bears and bows. It looked *good*, and three-year-old Abby was thrilled with how it turned out. Of course that *was* four years ago, more than half a lifetime to my daughter ....

"You know, you're right. Those bears do look sort of baby-ish. I guess you've been growing up, but your walls haven't. As kids get older, their rooms need to go through some changes too, and that's okay."

She sighed, looked up at me, then dropped her gaze briefly before making eye contact again and batting her lashes a bit. "And you know, *pink* isn't really my favorite color anymore, either."

Children grow, children mature, and their needs and desires change over time. I *know* that, yet it hadn't occurred to me that Abby had outgrown the bears on her wall, or the pink paint. Although I strive to be mindful of what's important to my children, it wasn't until Abby offered her feedback that I realized the need to recalibrate my understanding of her needs and wishes.

No matter how well we do our fathering job, what our children need from us today may not be what they need from us tomorrow. This isn't fickleness or indecision; it's simply development. There will be times when we're not the first one to recognize when such a transition is occurring. That's okay. Sometimes we'll become aware of it only through our child's discomfort or protest. That's why it's important to be receptive to their messages of discomfort or protest.

And that's why we're planning a trip to the paint store next weekend, to investigate shades of electric blue, Abby's *new* favorite color. I can't say I'm looking forward to another full day's work amidst drop-cloths and rollers. But if that's the price I have to pay for being blessed with a daughter who can express her needs so clearly and yet so considerately, I'm willing to do the work. Such labor – doing repairs, fix-ups, all in the service of indulging the wishes of our children – is an important component of fatherly love. Besides, if she's concerned that I'll be upset about something, but trusts our relationship enough to tell me anyway, I must be doing something right.

19

PACIFIERS

(Scribner)

♦

L ife transitions are a big deal. Especially for a child who feels things intensely. When Susan and I decided, based on some criterion that seemed important at the time, that it was time for Abby to bid farewell to her pacifier, we knew we were in for an ordeal. This child *really* liked her pacifier. We worked up to it gradually, first limiting pacifier use to her bed. She did eventually comply, but in the process of getting up each morning she'd still linger, sitting on the edge of the mattress, furtively taking those last few sucks, like a smoker huddled outside the theater at the end of intermission.

For the coup-de-grace, we adapted an idea we'd read about in a parenting magazine. We enlisted Abby's help in decorating a shoe box with bits of construction paper, glitter, drawings, etc.

We constructed a shrine to all the "baby things" she had relinquished in recent months, filling it with them: the old newborn-size onesies, her long-outgrown first pair of slippers, an old baby bottle complete with nipple and collar, an infant comb that could no longer compete with her thick wavy hair, a baby board-book that was too simplistic to hold her interest anymore.

With great ceremony, I held each item aloft and pronounced it a relic of her babyhood. Next, we gave Abby a chance to say a few words about or to the item, give it a good-bye hug and kiss, and place it in the box herself. Caught up in the festivities, she happily did all this – until she came to her pacifier. She gazed longingly at it, looked up at us and moaned, "But I really *love* my nuk-nuk."

"We know you do, sweetie" was our reply, loving but firm.

She bravely laid it to rest in the box, affixed the top, and asked to put the tape on all by herself. We applauded her courage and maturity, and her face brightened. We marched together, taking the box to a special "mausoleum" in the basement, ensuring that she'd know exactly where it was, and invited her to come down and visit it if she ever felt the need.

After a few nights of reassurance, hand-holding, and praise for being such a Big Girl, she moved on. She never did go down to visit the shrine.

And I only went twice.

You see, I *miss* her babyhood from time to time. Not *all* the time, mind you; I'm glad to be rid of many aspects of it – the diaper pail, the nightly production of mixing up formula bottles, the hours of colicky crying, having to be mindful of her whereabouts and actions *at all times* .... But every so often, I get a pang of grief, like a kick to the solar plexus, which signals a fleeting, deeper realization: *that* phase of her life – and mine – is gone forever. *That* relationship can never be re-captured.

Growth is a good thing. And being acutely aware of change, even just for a moment, enhances my appreciation of how transient my child's childhood is. The bittersweet feeling serves as a reminder that significant things are being lost, and therefore gained.

20

PACIFIERS: THE SEQUEL

(Scribner)

♦

After surviving the tribulations of the pacifier transition with Abby, I figured I was now uniquely prepared to handle that transition with Daniel. The time was clearly drawing near. Daniel had gotten into a routine of falling asleep with the pacifier in his mouth. Eventually, he'd enter the open-mouthed-snoring stage of sleep. In accordance with the laws of physics, when mouths open, pacifiers tumble to the floor of dark bedrooms. When that vacuum seal is broken, internal psychic alarms sound and Daniel wakes up. He notices that his mouth is vacant and cries out for help.

"Mohhhhh-me. MOHHHHHHH-ME. I no find my nuk-nuk."

Both parents wake up. Susan, whose reflexes are much quicker than mine at such cruel hours of the morning, goes in to assist. I lie in bed, waxing philosophical over the irony of our sleep being *disrupted* to retrieve an object meant to help our son (and therefore us) sleep.

Over the next few days, we began discussing strategies for The Transition. We hadn't yet finalized plans on this evening, as I rocked him before putting him to bed. "Where my nuk-nuk?" he asked at the appropriate moment in our going-to-bed ritual. I looked at the hallowed place on the shelf next to the rocking-chair. Not there. I looked on the floor. Under the chair. The tension mounted as I searched; he joined in. We were so *close* to making the transition, and now this crisis! I mentally calculated how long it would take to dash out to the 24-hour drugstore to pick up a fresh pacifier. It could work. But would he even *use* an unfamiliar one? And was there gas in the car? Did I have any cash in my wallet? Would he cry the entire time I was gone, upsetting his sister and mother? I had to risk it. I *had* to get him one, or we'd be up all night with him.

Sweating and panic-stricken, I looked at Daniel. Pouting, he repeated "Where my nuk-nuk?" Awash with shame and guilt, I broke the news to him.

"Daniel, I can't find your nuk-nuk anywhere. I think it's LOST."

"Lost?"

I braced myself for the explosion. My shoulders tensed. My jaw clenched. I leaned back, hoping to buffer the impact of the blast. I envisioned the years of psychotherapy he would endure because of this fateful evening. I cringed as he opened his mouth to speak.

"M-m-m-maybe we need to sleep without it." Matter-of-fact. He toddled over to his bed and climbed up. He began to pull the covers over himself. "I can do this all by my-self . . . First, the sheet ... next, the blanket."

I looked at him, astonished. He smiled at me. "Mommy showed me." He looked at me again, impatiently, I think. "Nite-nite. I want the light OFF." He turned on his side, snuggling with a stuffed animal as I stood there in disbelief.

"You're not mad at me?" I asked.

"NoooooO." Said with rising inflection, like a kindergarten teacher. "I not mad at you, Deeda. I happy at you. Nite-nite. I want the light OFF."

We often do our children a disservice when we project our expectations onto them. There's nothing wrong with trying to anticipate crises and being prepared for them, but it's just as important to remind ourselves that those expectations are only educated guesses, and that what is a struggle for one child may be inconsequential for the next. We fathers run the risk of projecting our own worries onto our children to the point that we *teach* them to make a big deal out of things.

Childhood rites of passage are dramatic – especially in the eyes of parents who have been counting the moments leading up to their occurrence. A child's first step or first word;

graduating from bottles, or pacifiers, or diapers; first day of school ... these are important events, occasions worthy of being marked. Each of them is a mixture of joy and trauma. We do well to prepare for the "trauma" part. But we need not become preoccupied with it. So, keep on preparing – but remember to remain open to surprises.

21

BECOMING A FATHER LATER IN LIFE

(Frey)

♦

MEMORY: I'm sitting with DiAnne in childbirth class. This is her first round, my third; but it's been awhile, nine years. I look around the room with equal shares of comfort and discomfort. I'm consoled by the fact that I have done this before; I'm experienced. Most of what the instructor is saying sounds familiar, old hat. Yet, I'm deeply disturbed by something else: I am literally old enough to *be* the father of the young father-to-be and pregnant woman sitting across from me. Often, I still consider myself to be a very young man. Folks with gray and white and blue hair still refer to me as "son." But I see that in this gathering I am the elder statesman. So, I begin to chew on a whole new set of self-doubts, not the inventions of a 24 year old first timer, but the anxious, semi-paranoiac ruminations of an older guy:

Who do I think I'm fooling? I'll be pushing 60 when my kid goes off to college. I can't keep up with a high energy boy (the knowledge of his gender already gleaned from the miracle of ultra-sound); I'll embarrass him. What was DiAnne thinking? She tricked me into having this kid. If she hadn't wanted a baby I'd be planning my next vacation, not sitting here like Keith Richards at a rock 'n' roll convention. How can I possibly wake up for midnight feedings at my age?

You get the general picture here, elder statesman on the outside, basket case on the inside.

Well, for the most part I'm a man of openness and honesty, so on one dark, unforgettable January night, in a moment of extreme clarity and total temporary insanity, I *told* DiAnne my thoughts *just* as I had been thinking them in their most unadulterated, juvenile form. I will tell her much later that if I could re-wind our marital clock and do one thing over, I would suck those words back in my mouth, knowing the deep hurt I inflicted. That is not to be.

This story reminds me that it's essential to be connected to my fear and to develop the skills for expressing that fear to caring and objective sources. It also reminds me of the havoc I can wreak as a partner, friend, or parent if I *dump* that fear in its rawest, most primitive form on my loved ones. My unfiltered fear often finds the light of day as anger, accusation, denial, and general childish nonsense. There's a better way.

BECOMING A FATHER LATER IN LIFE: PART II

As is often the case in my life, there was an opportunity for a re-test on the fear exam later in the childbirth process. DiAnne had a wild and woolly delivery and although the doctors would like to say there was never any real danger, we are both convinced that she came close to leaving us and passing to the other side. Previous experience went a long way in giving me the backbone to support her through the process. My love for her brought me to a level of focus that kept me by her side throughout (I didn't even notice all that blood until Nathan and DiAnne were safe in this world). I will later weep, alone and with a man I trust, as the delayed expression of my terror and relief. DiAnne and I will later share our fears, after she has physically healed from her trauma and had a chance to get to know our beautiful boy. I will feel absolutely *no* fear as I hold my third child for the first time. I *do* feel the same old fear the first time he cries incessantly, and a whole new *world* of fear the first time he has Croup. DiAnne and I will be simultaneously pleased and offended to be interviewed for a newspaper story on becoming parents "Later In Life." I will feel incredible joy as we sit for our picture; DiAnne, Carly, Aimee, Nathan, and me. It's all new. It's all the same.

The best news in that Nathan is almost six now; we've just come in from building a snow fort and within our regimen of wrestling, climbing, and

running he has no idea yet that his dad is an old guy
... he simply expects me to keep up. I'm wearing my
No Fear ball-cap as we play. Yeah, sure.

22

SAD, HAPPY DAYS

(Scribner)

◆

The episode of "Happy Days" had just ended. The one where Joanie declares her independence from her parents, and insists on going to Chicago. Her parents resisted, as they were having trouble letting go of her, trouble acknowledging that she had in fact grown into a mature young lady. In the end, they saw their shortsightedness and blessed her on her journey. My daughter Abby drank it all in. She looked up at me with those daisy-shaped eyes. Then she burst into tears.

"I'll never forget this episode for the rest of my life! I'm gonna be thinking about this episode every day for as long as I live...." She had grasped – deeply – the significance of it.

The fact that this episode aired when her mother was out of town for several days on a business trip served to magnify things further;

themes of taking leave and parting from parents gain in significance when they mirror real-life experience.

As she sobbed, I held her. I marveled that she had grasped the essence of the story at such an obviously deep, personal level. Then my energy began to shift, out of my head, downward, into my chest, my gut, and finally radiating out into my hands, which were engaged in that mesmerizing, automatic circular stroking that we do to soothe children or other loved ones. Then her sobs and wails caught my attention in a new way; their rhythm was disturbing, unsettling, ... familiar. I closed my eyes, trying to identify it.

Within seconds, I knew. My hands remembered. As they continued their soothing strokes, they led me back to Abby's infancy, when she cried for several hours on end every night, and I would yearn with all my heart and soul to comfort her, to soothe her, to bring her – and us --- some peace. The endless rocking, the pacing in the hallway with her, back and forth, back and forth; she, so tiny, helpless, and unhappy; me so large, caring, yet powerless.

The theme of the show – "little girls growing up" – suddenly thumped me in the chest. My eyes welled with tears as I opened them to see my hand stroking not a frantic, colicky infant, but a saddened, tortured soul of a schoolgirl, whose lanky frame no longer fits into my lap. Yet she was still inconsolably unhappy, and I was still powerless, despite my profound wish to soothe her.

"I just love that episode so much; I think I love it TOO much. I don't want to ever have to leave you and Mommy because I'm grown up." I reassured her that she'd never have to leave unless she was ready to, and that she can decide for herself when the time is right. "But what if I don't feel it's the right time, but you and mommy aren't around anymore, and I have to do it anyway?"

Can it be? A six-year-old child, able to telescope herself into the future, envision conceivable situations, and project herself emotionally into them? I hope, I pray that this is a sign of her intelligence and emotional sophistication. I fear, I dread that it's a sign of insecure attachment, the echoes of feelings of premature abandonment by her parents. Old pangs of guilt about our decision to use daycare re-surface.

I have no answers for her, nor for myself on these matters. So I just try to be there with her, physically, emotionally. Two sad souls abutting each other, one pitifully offering the weak consolation of a long-outgrown lap, the other awkwardly trying to fold herself into it, equals in their grief at the loss of childhood.

23

FIRST BOYFRIEND

(Frey)

♦

Dads obsess about this!

Oh sure, we laugh, offering scores of mirthless jokes and thinly veiled threats: *I'll ground her, until she's 30. He might be polite, but I know what he really wants: I was a teenage boy once. I'll just let him know about the fate worse than death that he faces if he touches her.*

You know what I'm referring to: your daughter's first boyfriend. He arrives at your doorstep, calling you by a name previously reserved for your father and grandfather, "Hi, Mr. .... " The centuries-old fear of fathers has come to rest in your castle, your little girl is growing up. You're quite sure she will date a young man as confused and hormonally charged as you were in adolescence – a terrifying thought. You may become protective, overcome by a sudden need to impart pearls of wisdom that you had somehow held back for the first 16 years of her development. You may become controlling, setting rules to cover the rules about your rules. A few poor misguided souls may even turn toward laissez-faire, giving her the freedom you weren't given at that tender age.

Whatever your response, you cannot – *I* cannot – stop the inevitable march of time and body chemistry:

The back door opens and in walks Carly, followed by a tall, handsome, friendly, *older* young man. In the back door, the *back* door, mind you ... you know, the door reserved for *family* ... close friends ... guests, *real* guests ... I mean ... well, I'm drifting a bit ....

After I recover from my well-disguised moment of shock, we move to the living-room. The next thing I know, Carly has flitted off to check out DiAnne's reaction to this young hunk; leaving the lad and myself alone. We sit and begin some manner of conversation. As we talk, I watch the young man warily, searching for signs of whatever horrors I'm concerned he may visit on my first born. Then a strange and unexpected feeling comes over me, one I can only describe as empathy. Suddenly, I am flashing back some 28 years to another living-room and another father; Joan's dad, who, while I await her final preparations for my inaugural date, is trying to convince me that my name can't be pronounced "Fry", it's spelled phonetically to be, "Fray" (One of many dismal memories of meeting the patriarchs of various dates). As I pull myself back into the present, I am surprised to feel the rumblings of a certain kinship with this young man who is threatening the very foundation of my life as a parent. I realize that he is no more excited about this moment than I am; I see in his face that there are a hundred places he would rather be right now than here, trying to chat with Carly's dad. I see this because we are kindred spirits; my spirit is simply a bit more weathered than his. And so, I resolve to push through my resistance of this addition to our circle and begin getting to know this fellow. As I do, I become aware of a deeper fear: that this rite of passage will bring sadness and hurt to my daughter, and that it is *her* time, not mine, to enter this stage of life.

Later, when I am alone, I will also touch my joy. Carly *glowed* tonight. A young woman, even my little girl, is gloriously beautiful in love, and I must admit that in her 16 year old way, she is in love. I will also be validated. DiAnne and I have created an atmosphere in which our daughter feels free to spontaneously bring her boyfriend to meet us; she is happy and wants to share this exciting time with us. And I will feel at least *some* sense of security, in that I trust who my daughter is and realize that my first impressions of this lad are favorable. I will sleep with all my feelings tonight: joy, fear, and sadness. Carly has arrived at a new stage in her development and so have I.

At some point, while discussing these changes with other adults, I will hear from several about the hurt Carly will probably experience in this relationship, about the possibility of *sex*, along with all of its emotional and physical risks. I understand these realities, and with the able guidance of my wonderful wife I have assisted Carly in facing and preparing for these realities. I refuse to panic; I refuse to obsess over that which I can no longer control. I will, however, worry. I will mess up and lecture Carly about all manner of parental concerns (Grandma Terry wanted me to be a preacher and although I did not have the calling in total, I am given to sermonizing). I will decide to open my home to the young men she dates; knowing them will tell me much about her.

As for Carly, she will have fun, feel pain, and ultimately experiencing the loss of this first love, that hurt we've all experienced and ache to shield our children from. She will also leave this first relationship for what I judge to be very solid reasons. She'll openly share her feelings about the decision, she'll grieve with those close to her, and she'll recover quite nicely. Then, she'll arrive at our door with the next young man, who shall remain anonymous to protect the privacy of what is still a happening combination at the time of this writing.

We have all learned. Thank God, because time marches on whether I evolve with grace or antagonism.

LEGACIES

Children have never been very good at listening to their elders, but they have never failed to imitate them.

-- James Baldwin

24

BLOODLINES

(Frey)

♦

I come from a long line of wheezing, hacking, coughing males. In years past, had you come calling on my family during the cold or allergy seasons, you would have been regaled with stories of my dad's childhood asthma and my mother's seemingly endless string of nights of holding and rocking the infant *me*, so that I could breathe a bit and grow into a wheezing, hacking, coughing toddler. I've grown quite tired over the years of these tales of childhood disease and heroic parent sacrifice; for crying out loud, I know the drill from both sides. I've *been* the little sick one *and* I've been the father of two daughters, one of whom has an admittedly less intense female version of these maladies. I also felt assured that I understood this struggle from the parental end of the telescope. I was more than certain that I saw the big picture.

And then came Nathan. You see, in confusion ... OK, ignorance ... OK, *arrogance*, I had failed to grasp the label "males" as a key word in this ancestral gift. So, I'm coasting along, the proud papa of a newborn son, oblivious to the possibility of having created my own personal rendition of "history repeats itself." Then it happens.

One starlit, chilly October evening, DiAnne and I are abruptly awakened by a terrifying sound emanating from Nathan's room, a sound like that of a small barking puppy. We rush in. Nathan cannot catch his breath; he's panic-stricken and we have no idea what's happening. Racing toward the hospital, hitting every red light and running it, we arrive at the ER and receive the diagnoses of Croup and RSV. In the next five years our little guy's autumns and winters will include a host of respiratory illnesses leading to hospitalizations, numerous moonlit ER visits, midnight drop-ins from the local EMT's complete with flashing lights, and hour upon hour of sitting by the steamy shower, barely awake, with hot water on full blast. And, of course, lots of trips to see the good Dr. Schlansky. As you may know, seeing IV tubes coming from the body of your infant child brings the fragility of life home to rest smack dab in the center of your heart. Children are resilient; but they are also delicate. For me, beyond placing a new value on the beauty of a full night's sleep, these times brought forth a newfound respect for the limitations of medicine and another powerful reminder of the incredible responsibility I took on when I decided to bring little humans into this world. These experiences also caused me to look again at my own parents, and in a quite different light (more on this in a moment).

Happily, up to now, Nathan has weathered each storm. As he grows older the frequency and severity of these episodes has diminished some, as the doctor said they would. I can see some emotional effects from these disruptions – a slightly increased fear of sleeping in his own bed, a stronger dependence on keeping a parent close by, dialogues about sickness, hospitals, God and death. All of these concerns make sense; I remember many of them from my own past. DiAnne and I understand the importance of sharing feelings and finding solutions to fear; our son is fortunate that we are attentive to those concerns. Oh, and just so I don't get complacent, the Natester has been experiencing some difficulties with his eyes that several physicians are currently struggling to diagnose. With faith and good fortune, I hope to write an essay on his excellent health soon.

I've received other gifts from Nathan's trials. I've connected more fully with my own childhood experience through Nathan and, as a psychotherapist, this has given me a greater sensitivity in assisting chronically ill clients, including many with more severe illnesses whose endings are not always as happy: Diabetes, Cystic Fibrosis, Lupus, mental illness. And finally, I now look at my parents and see that I really *didn't* get it. I now look at them, especially the mother who was my primary caregiver, and realize they *did* save my life, more than once. And a rich life it is. So here's to you mom and dad, and to all of you who care for a sick or disabled child every day; those of you who give not only physical care, but love and hope. I honor you. You are heroes with no press clippings.

ADDENDUM: Latest problem: headaches. But they have subsided; it's summer and Nathan is going full speed. Cool.

25

GRANDFATHERS (I)

(Scribner)

♦

We are defined, in part, by our origins. A man born in the deep South *is* a Southerner, and his identity will either be shaped by that fact, or shaped by his rebellion *against* that fact. In a similar way, we are defined in part by our parentage and ancestry. Depending on one's circumstances, this can be either a source of comfort or a source of turmoil and confusion.

In a more immediate way, we are defined in part by our fathers and grandfathers. My identity was shaped by my father in innumerable ways. This shaping occurred during the not quite 15 years that we coexisted on this Earth, but has undeniably continued since his death. While he was living, I was aware that we shared intellect – both intellectual ability and a propensity to define ourselves in terms of that ability – and that this was especially prominent in the area of language. He was an English teacher. I thrived in every English class I ever took, and set off to college fully intending to become an English major. We both thrived in the realm of words, and I believe we were both so caught up in the flow and swirl of the words inside our heads that we often neglected to bring those words out, to use them as a way of connecting with other people, including each other.

I knew this similarity existed, and never felt any particular discomfort about it. I do regret that it never became an explicit way for the two of us to connect. But I have seen that some sort of connection did occur. I was made aware of it when my mother learned of how I had proposed to my wife. Along with a fancy dinner and an engagement ring, I selected a poem and had it professionally typeset and framed for my wife-to-be. It was Ogden Nash's "Tin Wedding Whistle" – a whimsical yet touching piece about marriage. When I mentioned this to my mother, a look of reminiscence overtook her face, and she said "that's just the sort of thing your father would have done." This had an eerie impact on me. Sort of like when I look at the pictures from my parents' wedding, and see my father as a young man whom I resemble strongly.

I was made aware of this connection again while showing my mother some of the light verse I've had published. She thoughtfully read through the issue of *Light Quarterly* in which my latest poem appeared, gathered her thoughts, and proclaimed "your father would have loved this journal." She was referring to a journal that *I* love. It seems that as I get older, or perhaps the more I pursue my writing, I'm becoming more and more aware of my similarities to him. I'm encouraged by these links; they help heal my feelings of disconnection from my father.

And grandfather? Grandpa Scribner ... hard-working Congregationalist minister ... until *I* came along, the only Scribner with a doctorate (D. Div.) and a Phi Beta Kappa key ... yes, I feels some links to him as well. Pragmatic ... dry sense of humor ... tendency to be a bit rigid ... insistent on high standards for conduct in oneself and others ... yeah, there are some links there, all right. But I wonder if my father felt linked to this man.

My grandfather, you see, was not my father's natural father. Born to an unwed mother (a bright woman with thick, wavy hair, so the story goes), my father was adopted by the Scribners at a young age. Apparently blessed with a keen intellect, he was able to hold his own as the son of a serious intellectual. The rigidity and strictness which I understand to have characterized his upbringing may have been more troublesome; family lore has it that my father was "sent away to boarding school," (which in those days was most often done with "underachievers" or children with behavior problems), did well enough to matriculate at Yale (his adoptive father's *alma mater*), only to (in the words of a kind informant who responded to my requests for information about my father) "enjoy the newfound freedom of college a bit *too* much."

I wonder a great deal about what my father thought and felt about his own personal legacy. I myself have felt sad at not having known my father better, more intimately; but that struggle pales in comparison to my father's dilemma of never knowing who his natural father was – and of knowing that the man who reared him was *not* his father.

And, a generation later, the impact is a vexing one: I've been shaped by the man who fathered me; I share some of his qualities, as well as qualities of the man who raised *him*. But there once lived a man who is my grandfather – a man who impregnated a woman in Wisconsin, who for whatever reason did not marry her, and who never met the son he had sired. He might have been a skid-row bum; he might have been a famous writer who wanted to keep his dalliance a secret; he might have been a psychologist who wished he understood his own father better.

My mind spins, wondering as I sit here at my computer tonight who my natural grandfather was. Certain aspects of my lineage can be clearly traced to my father, and some of those to *his* father – but there the trail ends. That's frustrating and unsatisfying to me.   I can only imagine the frustration and dissatisfaction my father must have felt.

26

GRANDFATHERS (II)

(Frey)

♦

In my fifth effort to write about grandfathers I finally realize where I have been stuck: in my heart. You see, I believe strongly in the importance of grandfathers in a child's life. A grandfather's wisdom, love, and nurturing male energy can often balance the tension in father-child relationships. Yet, I could not write.

My beliefs are borne, in part, from what I have not lived; I have not loved my grandfathers in any deep way. I have no active memories of great-grandfathers, or of generations before them. And so, as I look toward my father's father and my mother's father to touch my deepest understanding of generativity, I find a void. Henry Frey surely loved me. He bought me tennis shoes, he gave me money for college. Yet, I never heard him speak the words to me, or even to his first born son, my father. Instead, I saw him lecture and ridicule and rage and work ... work ... work. I know my father loves his father deeply, he speaks of him as a good man. I have heard others, loyal employees for decades at The Factory owned by grandpa and dad, speak of him with respect and appreciation. I, however, have remained at a safe distance from Henry's memory, judging him from well beyond arm's length, sentencing him to a life-term as undeserving of my warmth or deep respect.

Adolph Hulka stands in an even harsher light in my recall ... vapor ... soulless ... in love with only himself; irresponsible husband and father; absent grandfather. Adolph never met my children. I have often blamed him for any, and all, significant pain in my mother's childhood. Although I have heard parts of his story – immigration, death of his father, adoption and loss of identity to a harsh step-father – I have held him in my heart with no forgiveness.

How then do I speak to the incongruity between my desire and my reality? I hunger for grandfather energy, and preach healing and forgiveness in my work – yet I have little warmth in my heart for my own grandfathers. How do I reconcile these contradictions? In the past I have assaulted the issue with little conscious understanding. The result was a confusing combination of dependence on the blessings and teachings of older, wiser men and a covert sabotage of any male authority who did not, in my judgment, live up to my expectations and fully validate my "specialness." I've been a tough guy to grandfather.

In the present, I have reached a new awareness and thank God for placing Bob Brundage, Stefan Ryback, and Jim Howard in my life; three men of dramatically different personalities who brought loving grandfather energy to me with one common characteristic; they each nurtured my developing manhood with equal parts love and challenge. Bob, who told me I was "wise" beyond my years and, concomitantly, taught me what I *didn't* know as I played co-therapist with him. Bob, who taught me loving confrontation, who brought Big Macs back to our country hospital from his consultations in the big city; who spoke in wise parables to clients and then winked at me, as if he and I truly shared their special meanings. Dr. Ryback (even now I have difficulty writing "Stefan," always feeling as though his first name truly was Doctor), whose harsh manner and condescending attitude barely hid his unflagging willingness to teach a very green young man who was hungry to learn and, when challenged with love, hungry to please. Jim, who remains my close friend, has heard every secret of my past, has stood by my side at two dozen men's workshops and blessed my leadership potential, and has helped me tend the fire of my passion for leading men in healing their spirits. With these teachers I have learned and I have laughed. From these men I have seen what being a mentor, an elder, a grandfather can be about in this world.

I honor any man, any grandfather, who is reading these words and is sending his loving energy to his grandchildren and to the grandchildren of other men. There are many wonderfully nurturing grandfathers in this world, my children have Harold Frey and Lorne Slemp and Jim Howard, men I am grateful for. Further, I honor any younger man who has given the loving elder in his life the respect, time, and listening ear that he so richly deserves.

As for myself, I believe it is time to heal my relationships with the blood grandfathers I was given, Henry and Adolph. It is time to accept who they were, why they were, and to accept the love they had to give. It is time to call upon the men of my circle to assist me in growing up ... again. None of my elders has been perfect – not Bob or Jim or dad, not Henry or Adolph. I have learned that only my compassion will move me out of my judgment and anger. I have learned to trust that through this healing of my past resentments I bring new life to my present and future. Perhaps I will become more expressive of my gratitude to the grandfathers of my children. Perhaps I will be blessed with some knowledge that can only be seen when I get to the other side of this work. Perhaps I will find love for the grandfathers who gave me what they had to give.

Perhaps I will prepare for my time as grandfather.

27

RESEARCHING MY FATHER

(Scribner)

♦

Join now in the chorus of the American male: "I
didn't really know my father very well." As it is
for a lot of men, this is true for me. But one day
it dawned on me that I was bothered by this, and felt
that the gaps in my knowledge about him were
holding me back in some way. I resolved to do
some research to fill in those gaps. Coincidentally,
at that time I was re-reading Sam Osherson's
Finding Our Fathers, a book which contains the
statement (on p. 206) "one way of healing the
wounded father is to plunge into your father's
history. A man needs to find ways of empathizing
with his father's pain." As I read, I realized this was
exactly what I was seeking to do. As a father
myself, I could *imagine* the pain and helplessness of
being unemployed, of not knowing where the
mortgage payment was going to come from, and of
eventually turning to the mother-in-law for help. I
could only start to *imagine* what it's like to be father
to ten children, and to honor one's vow to see them
all college-educated. But what was it like for *him* to
go through that? And how did his doubts, his fears,

manifest themselves? And how did he come to terms with them?

I had already gleaned what insights I could from *within* the family; it was time to cast my net wider. My mother was able to provide me with names and addresses for some of my father's relatives and college friends, people with whom she still exchanges Christmas cards. I sent out numerous letters, asking people to write back with their recollections and impressions of my father, especially regarding his basic character. I received many gracious and well-intentioned replies, most of which encouraged me in my efforts. One respondent, however, a college roommate of my father's whom I've never met, wrote back to upbraid me. He presumed that I was looking for shortcomings in my father that I could use to excuse shortcomings in myself. He said that whatever my father's shortcomings might have been (and they remained nameless), he was a good man who cared deeply for me and all his children, and I was lucky to have him as a father, as I could certainly have done much worse. After a brief digression against the process of "blaming parents" (I believe he was put off by my mentioning that I'm a psychologist, a profession which he appeared to hold in low regard), he did describe my father as "the most phlegmatic person I've ever met."

This respondent then suggested a few other people I might contact, people who "knew him better." As the responses trickled in, I noticed a pattern. Each person made an earnest effort to provide some information about my father, usually in the form of anecdotes. Each apologized for their contribution being so meager, and closed by suggesting that there was another person, or a few other people whom I should contact, as these others "knew your father better." It was only after most of the letters were in that I realized this was the one feature they all had in common –each respondent felt there was someone *else* better suited to the task of telling me what my father was really like. Not one of them would own up to feeling that he or she "knew him the best." I was on the verge of concluding that no one did.

But then the mail brought what turned out to be the final reply to my inquiries – a blessing, a gold mine, seven solid single-spaced pages from a man who cautioned in his introductory paragraph that *"for the forty years I knew your father, he was one of my great, good friends. There are only so many friends of that sort that you make in your whole life, and he was one of those, and I see him through that prism."*

This letter overflowed with anecdotes, images, and recollections that filled my heart and repeatedly brought tears to my eyes. I began to feel like an idiot for not being able to summon up such images myself; the man described sounded so warm and caring that he'd stand out in the mind of anyone who had ever known him. Many of the comments dealt with his ease and comfort as a father: *One of the remarkable things about your father was that, unlike most men, he just absolutely loved babies. Nothing was too much trouble for him. He cuddled; he changed diapers; he cooed and he crooned. This vision is my most enduring vision of him because I saw him do it with many a child.*

The letter closed with this summation: *"My memory of him will always be of a very big man holding a very small baby, and being relaxed and happy, not tense, no hidden agenda -- a good guy, a good friend."*

Through my research, I *was* able to empathize with a bit of my father's pain. People shared bits about his struggle to support a large family, about his struggle to live up to the expectations of his minister-father, about his alcoholism. But every account of him was distinctly tilted in a complimentary direction; even if he wasn't know intimately by many people, he was liked by most.

In my research, I also learned about my father's strengths. I rejoice especially in our common quality of love for children. I guess I come by it honestly.

When I began my research on my father, I was feeling disconnected. No longer disconnected, I'm left feeling sad, sad that I cannot remember him better. And in my sadness, I am connected to my father. For, in addition to my sadness at not knowing him well, I feel sad that he did not know *me* well. Like him, I'm not easy to get to know. I try to remedy this in my life, in my writing, and in my family, by revealing my heart. I want my children to *know* me, just as I am devoted to knowing *them*.

28

BECOMING MY DAD

(Frey)

♦

It's hard to believe I can remember, let alone retell, the silly jokes dad used to recite, and sing the silly songs he used to sing over and over, as we pretended each time was the first.

I look in the mirror. I have a different hair color, different glasses, many different features, yet I still see *him* looking back at me. I think of the joke that old dogs and their masters begin looking alike ... I guess older dogs and their fathers do, too. I'm not him, I only look, sound, think, feel, sing, act like him ... at times. No doubt my father hopes I am a slightly improved model, taking the best and leaving the rest. I hope the same for my children.

I have known many men with scores of negative images of dad, men who are immersed in their childhood pain, whose life mission has been to become *nothing* like their fathers. Impossible. In fact, the rage, shame and fear that creates this absolute rejection *of* father emulates the rage, shame and fear created *by* father, spawning the man's exact worst nightmare ... "Like father, like son." It is my experience that the man who walks into my office with the above objective is often the only person in his life who doesn't know how much like dad he has become. Should you, like that man, chose not to walk in the footsteps of your father, you will need much more than anger, denial and rejection; you will need a place and people to help you heal and change. You will need time and a fierce commitment to rigorous honesty about the ways you *have* followed in dad's footsteps. You will need to reach acceptance of this man as your father.

I have also met some men whose mission is to be *just* like dad. Impossible. I was born with a degree of uniqueness and have succumbed to many other influences since that first moment; so have we all. In seeking to be *be* dad a man will lose his dreams, or lose himself. Should you chose to emulate your father, a wonderful choice for many of us, you will still need to put your own personal stamp on your manhood. This, too, will take time.

You see, I'm not my father; I just tell the same silly jokes and sing the same silly songs over and over – in *my* voice, which sounds a lot like his, but not exactly like his. How do I know this? Recently, for the first time since I was a child, dad and I sang in the church I was raised in. While accepting compliments for a job well done from folks who remembered me as a much smaller person, I reflected on how much my voice tone that day had mirrored dad's as we sang. I could close my eyes and almost hear us as one ... almost. And I loved that. I loved the gift of being able to sing with him, in my own slightly different voice, after 30 some years.

And so, I walk a path of being the same as, and different from, my father. Powerful. Humbling.

29

FACES OF MOM AND DAD

(Scribner)

♦

I remember playing with my mother's face as she sat on the side of my bed to tuck me in at night. I would pull her cheeks, move her eyebrows up or down, and she would hold her face in the position I had put it. She would puff her cheeks out and let me squeeze them, to make them deflate. She was silly. She let me be silly. I didn't want it to end. It was light-hearted, frivolous, funny. She let me run the show – I controlled her face. It was power, but a power to create fun. It always surprised me that she would permit me to be so silly and to laugh, so close to bedtime. When I finally did lie down to sleep, my belly vibrated with a warm, joyful feeling.

I don't remember my father speaking to me directly in conversation. I remember angry, critical looks from him, but not words. When he was angry, he'd puff out the part of his face between his nose and his upper lip, with his lips pressed tightly together. "The Bulldog Face," my brother and I would call it. But words directed at me, I do not recall.

I remember being enraged at my daughter. I was trying to contain it, but ended up slamming things, yanking things, moving in an attenuated frenzy. With fear in her voice, she asked me "Deeda, why are you doing everything fast?" I told her "because I'm angry with you, and that's what I do when I'm angry." I calmed a bit. I was glad I had answered her question. I remember a previous time when she had asked the same question and I yelled at her. I remember seeing her face melt into tears of hurt and fear, and seeing the sobs rise from her chest up to her throat, then to her eyes. Reaching out blindly through her tears, she tried to hug me. I hate that I would hurt someone who so desperately needs my love, deserves my love.

30

GOLF

(Frey)

♦

My father gave me golf, with its chilled, dewy mornings and its fog hovering over the fairways as the summer sun comes into full view. He gave me club selection, and "keep your head down," and "smooth, easy swing."

My father gave me golf etiquette, which, with minimal adjustment, is life etiquette: "replace your divot ... we'll let these folks play through ... mark your ball but don't walk across the other man's lie on the green ... don't cheat ... we're just playing for fun today, so take a mulligan."

My father and golf gave me hope: "a couple of good putts and you'd have had a great round ...

you keep hitting that 4-wood and you'll be shooting par ... tough round, we'll get 'em next round."

My father and golf even gave me accountability:

I'm perhaps 14 years old, playing nine holes with Tim, my cousin, buddy and serious golf competition. I'm using my Uncle Bob's clubs. They are good clubs, but it's a bad round. Somewhere in mid-round I prepare my approach shot to the green. I choose a 5-iron ... I address the ball ... relax ... head down ... swing ... follow through ... clunk, shank, splash ... water shot. Aargh!!! The club leaves my hands, by way of me throwing it, and is propelled into the sky like a blade that lost its helicopter, as I simultaneously beg the Great Father to manifest a miracle, turn the clock back five seconds, and return that club to my offending hands. Too late. In one of those "what are the odds of this ever happening" moments, the club spins all the way to the green, hits the pin, and snaps off right between the shaft and the head. I don't recall my exact reaction, but I imagine it was something on the order of a churning stomach and an "Oh, s..t."

No amount of masking tape and Elmer's glue would fix that club. I retrieved the dismembered and dishonored stick and half-heartedly finished the round.

As I am writing this story, my first impression is that I returned to my aunt and uncle's home that afternoon with more than a little fear of my parents' response to my violence on the links. Looking deeper, I can connect with the great sense of embarrassment that I carried in the door. I had desecrated a sacred place, the golf course. I had destroyed a sacred, ceremonial object and on top of all that, it was one borrowed from a respected elder. But worst of all, my momentary lapse of conscious control exposed a piece of my dark side, my Shadow (as the Jungian psychologists label it); an aspect of my personality that I believed I had previously kept well hidden: my impulsive and explosive anger.

I prepared for my father's anger, which could be formidable. I'm sure I told my story with as much truth as I could muster, although I have no clear memory of this humiliation. Then, as I awaited my father's wrath, dad breathed, looked at me and calmly asked, "You have a 5-iron in your set, don't you?" "Yes." "Well, now that club is Uncle Bob's 5-iron." Maybe more was said, maybe not. I truly don't even remember relinquishing the club formerly known as Chris' 5-iron. Frankly, I'm not even certain this incident took place quite like I've recited it to you. None of that matters. What matters is that in my memory, in that moment, I received from my father a crucial lesson in accountability, a lesson that has stayed with me always. I have not always *lived* the lesson, but when I have, it has guided decisions of great import in my career, my marriage, my fathering. The message: A man had given a boy his trust. The boy, struggling to become a man, had literally and figuratively broken that trust and there had to be a cost; a personal price to be paid that had meaning in the boy's life.

Since that time I've wounded others with my anger. But, I've returned many times to the lesson given to me by golf, and dad, that day. Since that day, and thanks to the assistance of other good men and women, I have gotten better and better at thinking before I act or attack, owning my errors, cleaning up the emotional messes I occasionally make, and making amends to those I have harmed.

So, some of you have thought that golf is just a game, and a fool's game at that. No, golf is a sacred ceremony with much wisdom for those who will listen. Golf is sensual and spiritual and chock-full of life's best rules. Accountability is one of them. If I hunch up my left shoulder, I *will* slice. If I break a man's 5-iron, I will give him mine. This type of justice is often painful, and in our world hard to find, but it can be found ... on fairways and greens, in sand traps and thick, green rough.

I'm looking forward to teaching Nathan to golf. I hope I am able to gift its lessons to the next generation.

31

RITE OF PASSAGE

(Scribner)

♦

PROLOGUE:

A *s I've mentioned, my firsthand recollections of my father are very limited. I regard the following story as some mixture of fact and fiction. I cannot say that the events described below ever happened; nor can I say that they did not. What I do know is that the story bubbled up for me quite clearly one day when I set my heart toward the task of trying to recapture something good that arose from my relationship with my father. The father depicted arose from my imagination. But the contents and capabilities of my imagination reflect what I have experienced. What is reflected in this story, as well as in my own fathering efforts, is some sort of connection to my father – a blessing, an acceptance, an appreciation of the impact of fatherly benevolence.*

... Soon Phil drifted into the memory of receiving his first baseball glove on the day he turned eight years old. It was a Friday, memorable because his father arrived home from work early, with a present tucked under his arm. His father had calmly watched him unwrap it before taking Phil by the hand and leading him down the basement steps, into the sweet, musty smells of mildew and sawdust emanating from the hallowed space that was the Workshop. Phil's eyes stretched with awe as he gazed up at the glimmering tools hanging on the wall, dangerously sharp and beautiful. The union between his hand and his father's grounded him from the jolts of fear the sight of the jagged, pointed objects gave him. With a warm grip, his father steadied him while searching wordlessly among the sacred implements and potions arrayed chaotically on the workbench. "Now, I know it's around here somewhere ..." his father muttered. Phil swelled with anticipation as he wondered what was in store for him. Even without knowing, he felt the weighty importance of this moment. He was rarely permitted to come down to the Workshop. Whatever was about to happen, it felt like a rite of passage.

"Ah, there you are." His father raised a bottle of amber liquid, measuring its level with his eyes. "That'll probably be enough for at least one more glove."

"What's that stuff, Dad?"

"This? *This* ... is Neatsfoot Oil – the most important stuff to have when you get a new glove. You got to break the glove in before you can use it. Here ..." His father took the glove. He unscrewed the bottle's top and withdrew the strange-looking applicator, a handle and shaft of braided steel wires, like on a bottle brush, and what looked like a thick cotton ball at the end. After dunking the cotton ball back into the liquid, his father pulled it out, and proceeded to rub it on the palm of the baseball glove, dabbing and brushing, an artist before his canvas. After the leather had darkened a few shades, he handed the glove back to Phil.

Phil inhaled the strange, musky, manly aroma. He gazed at the moist leather, wondering what was to happen next. Looking up expectantly at his father, he opened his mouth to speak, but was cut short.

"Well, don't just stand there – rub it in!"

"Rub it in?" Phil parroted. His eyes searched the Workshop. "Um ... with what?"

"With what? Your *hand* – what else? I swear ... your mother's got you scared of doing *anything* that you might have to clean up after."

After looking at his father a bit longer to reassure himself that this was no joke, Phil stroked the lightly greasy surface of the glove with his fingertips, then with the length of his fingers, then with his whole hand. "Really work it in there, boy." Phil paused, took a deep breath, then let himself go, massaging the glove enthusiastically, kneading it with the heel of his hand, pressing hard with his fingers, then tracing his initials in the oil with his fingernail, then mauling the glove again with his palm, with his knuckles, finally pounding the pocket with his fist until his hand tired.

"What you do now is get your ball, tuck it in the pocket of the glove and get one of those wide rubber bands, and wrap it around the glove. That molds it to the shape of the ball. And if you want to break it in a little faster – this is the *real* secret – you slip it under your mattress for a few nights and sleep on it."

It finally made sense to Phil. To get the glove into shape, you had to be a little rough with it. It's cowhide; it can take it. He tucked it under his mattress, beneath where his hips would rest, to give it maximum weight while he was sleeping.

That night he chuckled to himself, recalling the story of the Princess and the Pea. Unlike the princess, he was *choosing* to sleep on this lump; the masculine code required it. And unlike the princess, he slept very well, and dreamed of diving to his left and to his right, snaring low line drives, tumbling deliciously in the infield dirt.

32

MALE MOTHERS

(Frey)

◆

T hanks to my mom, I can iron my shirts, sew a button, run a washing machine, and cook a tasty spaghetti sauce. Thanks to mom *and* dad I can hug my children, hug another man, hold a crying child, hold a crying adult, *be* a crying adult. I have learned, rejected, and re-learned that the ability to be soft does not diminish my capacity to be tough when necessary. I have learned that nurturing, care-taking, serving, and emoting are not the exclusive purview of the feminine. I have learned ... well, allow me to tell a story:

Today, I am at home instead of in the usual Thursday haunt, my counseling office. I'm taking care of Nathan through this autumn's first episode of the Croup. As I watch him in slumber restlessly on the sofa, I am touched by the spirit of my mother, miles away in Ohio, and of my wife, who is across town giving love to the homeless children of other parents. My mom held me day after day, night after night in childhood as I struggled to breathe. And if that weren't enough for one man's lifetime, in our fourteen years together DiAnne has taught me more about patience, unconditional love, and the joy of parenting than any man could hope to learn from one teacher.

So, as I sit with one of my three beloved kiddos, I am moved by the gentle side of my nature to lay my pen down and go to him; I adjust his blankets, brush his hair aside, and place my lips to his forehead in the time-honored ritual of testing for fever. I know that on another day we will prefer to wrestle, play Ninja Warriors, look at the car engine (with *both* of us imagining we know what we're doing), or stomp in the creek behind our house. Another day we will do an aggressive masculine dance, growling, conflicting, wills clashing, teeth gnashing. Today, though, Nathan opens his eyes in sleepy recognition, burrows deeper into the blanket, and returns to his dreams.

Sadly, our culture suffers from an epidemic of absent fathers. Many mothers are attempting, beyond any reasonable expectation, to learn the arts of mothering *and* fathering. Perhaps it is the strong Male Mother that I have come in contact with that gives me the vision of a nightmare land without fathers, where children are only formed as halves. This nightmare calls upon me, softly but with great power, to be a daily, loving presence in the lives of my children. I have so often left my beloved in the hands of a mother, or another, for their care. Today, I must call on the memories not only of my mother and DiAnne, but of my father and my mentors, of the dozens of warm, gentle, strong fathers that have served as my role models over four plus decades. Today, I'm home. I recommend it.

PAIN AND JOY

Parenthood is not an object of appetite or even desire. It is an object of will. There is no appetite for parenthood; there is only a purpose or intention of parenthood.

--R. G. Collingwood

33

CRISES

(Scribner)

♦

Today, I took my 5 year-old daughter Abby to her cardiologist. It's an annual ritual, one which always takes me back to that night when she was an infant and we were first made aware of her problem. Our pediatrician was performing his routine two-week post-natal well-baby examination of her; he placed his stethoscope to her tiny chest, and made the face of bad news. He drew in a long breath, abruptly ended the examination, and instructed us to take her to the emergency room immediately. We spent most of the night there trying to soothe a hungry, sleep-deprived infant enough for the doctor to do an EKG and Echocardiogram. For the Echo, the patient needs to lie perfectly still. But she was in a strange place, in the middle of the night, and she was hungry. She cried and squirmed. Drawing on our pitiful two weeks' worth of parenting experience, Susan and I took turns wrestling with the guilty, cruel feeling that comes with forcibly restraining a tiny baby – *our* baby – from moving. Her cries echoed through the strangely quiet halls of the ER; it seemed we were the only people there. The cardiology resident, sleepy and disheveled after being roused from sleep by his pager, was very patient and understanding, and finally got a usable reading.

Then he told us that our daughter has a hole in her heart.

Despite his efforts at compassion, the resident's summation came across as coldly clinical: "Keep an eye on her for signs of anoxia, breathlessness, or fatigue, and pre-medicate her with antibiotics whenever she has any invasive procedure to the alimentary canal or has any kind of dental procedure." The good news was that there was no imminent health risk, and that this kind of heart defect "usually" grows closed *within a year or two*.

Here we are today, a month and a day shy of her *fifth* birthday. This will be her fourth Echocardiogram. Each year, the hole has gotten smaller. But each year the hole has remained. Last year, her doctor mentioned the possibility of "surgical closure" – heart surgery – if the hole did not close up spontaneously. "How long do we give it?" was my question. She indicated that in Abby's case it *was* taking longer than usual to close up. She didn't give any clear answer to the question of how long we give it.

As with all the previous cardiologist visits, I spent the time there with my own heart full of caring, concern, and fear. *Abby's* fear showed only in subtle ways: poignantly and uncharacteristically wanting to sit on my lap while I read to her in the waiting room; clinging extra-tight to the special stuffed animal she'd brought along. Most of the time, she transcended that fear – playing rhyming games with me as we awaited the doctor's arrival, or gently flirting with the resident, or concentrating her efforts on faithfully and seriously carrying out the young doctor's request to "take a BIG, DEEP breath."

I sense that she knows, despite *my* best efforts to appear calm and low-keyed, that these visits are a big deal. I was scared for her. But more than that I was proud of her. Seeing her bravely lying on the Echo table, asking nothing more than "will you just hold my hand, Deeda?" brought tears to my eyes. So grown up, yet still so little and so trusting; so secure in her dependence on her daddy, and on those to whom he extends *his* trust.

I was loving her, utterly, completely. Nothing else – not the work stresses I was to face two hours hence, not my mother's ongoing struggles to care for my increasingly-demented grandmother, not even my dear friends who are about to face radiation and chemotherapy for their two-year-old son – entered my mind. For a while, nothing else existed for me. I was feeling Father-love. All-encompassing, fiercely-protective, I-would-die-for-you love.

Mercifully, today's appointment is quick; this time, the simple, old-fashioned stethoscope exam reveals to our doctor's knowing ears that the hole "is only very, very tiny now." She orders a repeat Echocardiogram just for good measure. Then she tells us that she now believes that surgery will never be needed; even if the hole does not close any further, Abby would be able to live worry-free, except for the quirk of needing those prophylactic antibiotics whenever she visits the dentist. As we leave, Abby looks up at me and asks "what does 'antibiotics' mean?" Stunned by her curiosity and her grasp of the significance of conversation intended to pass over her head, I knelt down to give her an extra hug and told her I'd explain it to her on the way to the car.

Before we can leave, a young couple comes in – first the mother, looking weary and stressed, still bearing the stomach of a woman who gave birth only two weeks ago, holding the tiny pink baby; next, the father, looking awkward and pale, lugging the over-stuffed diaper bag, over-eagerly extending a cold, clammy hand as he introduces himself to me. I make the obligatory small talk: how old is she, what's her name. He says they're here to have an Echocardiogram done. He looks panic-stricken. He welcomes Abby's light-hearted banter. He's kind and responsive to her, charmed by her distinctively nonsensical preschool brand of humor. He's trying not to let the nervousness show and she, knowingly or not, is doing everything in her power to help him relax. I figure that's supposed to be *my* job, as the more experienced dad here. I tell him that Abby had her first Echo when she was just two weeks old, too. "And as you can see, she's doing okay now." He laughs, feeling reassured, I hope.

34

STITCHES, OR, THE CIRCLE OF LIFE

(Frey)

◆

It's summer; I'm 10 or 11 years old. My brother Kevin and I are over at the Wasserman's. I'm standing in the yard; Kevin is proudly carrying his new toy lawnmower down the cement steps that lead from their back door. Suddenly his feet fly skyward and he comes crashing down, back of head first, onto the concrete. The next thing I remember is seeing mom and dad standing over him, and seeing Kevin's head laid open and the blood flowing. There's a trip to the hospital in Kevin's immediate future.

It's Easter weekend; I'm 42 years old. Dad and mom are in town for the holiday. Nathan is 5 years old. He follows DiAnne upstairs, making sure she doesn't get too far from sight. Moments later I hear another crash, and a scream of pain. My adrenaline sends me up the stairs two at a time to find Nathan already in DiAnne's arms, with a wet towel on his face, his little chin laid open, and blood flowing. We leave Carly and Aimee in the care of my parents and rush to the van, knowing a trip to the emergency room is in order. DiAnne gives me driving instructions as my fear causes me to miss the turn which would take us most quickly to the hospital. We both pay attention to Nathan's panic, speaking calmly, assessing his condition.

We arrive and the decision is quick: stitches. The nurses are kind. The doctor, the only male in the process other than me, is efficient but detached (I'll later wonder what that means). DiAnne constantly reassures Nate, holding his hand. I stroke his legs, repeating "I'm here, buddy," over and over, like a mantra of reassurance to both of us. Promising myself not to zone out, I listen to the heart-wrenching and courageous whimpers of my son as the doctor anesthetizes and sews his wound. I watch the entire procedure, seeking to understand my son's pain. He weathers this storm with tears and strength.

Later that night, watching Nathan sleep, I will try to feel guilty. I did not immediately respond when Nate panicked as the nurses tried to wrap him in a sheet to hold his body steady for the procedure. I will be reminded by those close to me that this is my first foray as a parent into the world of stitches and, by the looks of Nathan's face and the sounds of his heart as he talks of the trauma, he will heal well.

The next day, dad will reminisce about the various blows to the heads of my brother and sister through childhood. Miraculously, that part of *my* body seemed to escape serious physical damage. I will appreciate dad's honesty as he recalls his panic at the time of Kevin's fall and take in his validation as he compliments me on what he views as my calm handling of Nathan's accident. He will remind me of the resiliency of children. I will consider what I learned from the experience – that my son is a boy of great courage; that I practice what I preach, allowing my children to express their fear and tears, thereby reducing the emotional trauma of a scary situation; that each time I have faced my own fear and pushed through it I have become a better father.

I have seen and heard a lot of fear projection from fathers to sons in my therapy career: "Don't be such a baby, it doesn't hurt that bad" ... "You're really brave, you didn't cry at all." Well, that night I looked into my son's open wound and I looked into his eyes and I say: Yes, sometimes it does hurt that bad and a boy (or man) can be brave and weep.

How do I know these truths? My son taught me.

35

YELLING

(Scribner)

♦

Tonight, I yelled at my children. They were at the dinner table with me, doing playful, silly, moderately noisy things to each other. I asked them to stop, as the playing was keeping them from eating, and the noise was bothering me. They each muttered a cursory "okay," then resumed their playing. Again, I asked them to stop, somewhat more firmly. They responded in the same way, waited a few moments longer, then resumed their playing. I felt anger rising through the trunk of my body, into my throat and lungs. I said, in a voice that surprised even me with its depth and volume, "STOP DOING THAT, *RIGHT NOW!*"

They stopped immediately, turned to look at me, their faces frozen. Then, my daughter's face melted into an expression of clear, distinct fear. My son, the younger of the two, looked back and forth between her and me. My daughter rose from the table, excused herself, and walked toward the staircase; I thought I heard a sniffle as she made her way upstairs.

Waves of shame washed over me; I knew what she was feeling and what she was doing. She was fleeing from something that frightened her – me. I glanced at my son, half fearing, half hoping that he would give voice to the wrongfulness, the injustice of what I'd just done. That was too much to expect of him; what he gave me instead was his pure, raw experience of what I'd just done to *him*: "Deeda, when you yelled, I heard it echo."

I began apologizing, in as many ways as I could think of, and reflected back to him that my "echoing" yell must have been scary for him, which he confirmed. As I began my next layer of apologies to him, my daughter came back in. She took her seat at the table and glanced up at me with a pout on her face. I sensed that *she* was about to apologize for her part in "provoking" my outburst (ah, I've trained her well), so I intervened to block that. This one was *my* wrongdoing, and I could not bear to let her even begin to take the fall for it. Yes, she had been "annoying," and yes, she had failed to honor my several, better-modulated requests to "stop." But the wrong that *I* committed far outweighs whatever the two of them had been doing. They were being kids, being playful, and being more interested in having fun than in eating. But my actions were excessive, intimidating, and – worst of all – struck fear, even terror, in their hearts. I apologized to her. I "owned" the inappropriateness of my response, and took pains to let them know that it was out of proportion to what had occurred. I asked if there was something I could do to help them see that I do not hate them, to see that I'm safe to be around, and to re-connect with them. I was prepared to accede to any demand they might have come up with. Anything.

My daughter spoke first: "Can the three of us all do something together?" Then my son chimed in: "Yeah ... can we all play that computer game on the computer?"

To my relief, they were willing to welcome me back, asking of me only a very simple, token "make-up." To my chagrin, they were not prescribing a laborious penance, which might have allowed me to work so hard that I'd feel like I'd truly "paid" for my misdeed. Instead, they welcomed me back into their hearts, and at the same time left me to find my own way through my shame at the pain I had inflicted on them. Doing it the way they did it actually kept my inner spotlight on that shame for a while longer, for me to wrestle with. That's uncomfortable. It's hard, painful work for me. It's also absolutely *necessary* work for me, as it reduces the likelihood that I'll repeat this scene in the future.

Of course, remaining mired in shame is no way to live life. I've learned *that* the hard way, too. But this interaction with my children offers me a perplexing and healing resolution: my shame and regret linger long enough to change me, but are then neutralized by the forgiveness and acceptance my children offer. Those children model a capacity for acceptance that I hope to cultivate myself.

36

SMILEY, HAPPY PEOPLE

(Frey)

♦

I know a man, a passing acquaintance, who always smiles and says hello, always waves as he drives by. He's extremely polite. On occasion, in the quiet of a summer's evening, when our windows are open to the muggy St. Louis breeze, I have also heard the sound of his loud, rageful voice rocketing through the neighborhood. He has children and a wife, who would seem to be the recipients of this verbal barrage.

I know the man's son, a passing acquaintance. *He* always smiles and says hello; one of the most polite adolescents I've met in recent times.

I fear someone is going to get a load of anger from that lad someday.

37

HOW TO GET GREAT KIDS

(Frey)

♦

Sometimes I feel as if I have a flashing neon sign on my chest that reads "Psychotherapist: Have Empathy, Will Travel." People just seem to know they can talk to me about their lives. Maybe my face shows interest, concern. Maybe I listen well, ask incisive questions. Maybe I emit a scent only recognizable to those in need.

Anyway, I'm walking through the parking lot of the neighborhood grocery, headed toward my car. I notice that the young man loading his groceries into the pickup truck next to my vehicle has a sparkle in his eyes, eyes which are trying to make contact with mine. I lead:

"How's it going?"

"Great. Hey, I just found out my wife is pregnant again!"

"Congratulations. Kids are wonderful."

"Thanks ... Hey, I was wondering ... My son is great, easy, sleeps all night, and we have a lot of fun. But my friend told me a while back that if you get a great kid the first time, the next one's going to be a terror. What do you think?"

"I think that if your friend believes that, his next kid will probably be a terror, he'll make sure of it. I have three great kids. They're all different, but I don't have any terrors."

"So you really think the next one could be OK?"

"Absolutely."

"Thanks ... that's great!" As the guy turns to get into his truck, I hear him whistling.

This is *not* a Brady Bunch episode; this happened. And you know what? As I drove home, I was whistling too -- an upbeat little number; a song for my good fortune in meeting the man whose name I did not get, but whose love and excitement for his born and unborn children was contagious. Fatherhood is a miracle ... and all the kids can be OK.

38

GOOFY DADS

(Frey)

♦

I am second generation goofy. As I've shared before, my dad has jokes that I've heard a dozen ... a hundred ... a thousand times. He does impressions of Donald Duck, spontaneously breaks into song and (to mom's horror) burped at the dinner table when I was a child ("you did so, dad!"). After the transition from rapt attention to tolerance to annoyance, over the years I've arrived at a time in my development when I ... tell jokes my kids have heard dozens ... hundreds ... thousands of times:

Knock, Knock

Who's there?

Interrupting cow

Interrupting co ...

MOO, MOO, MOO

I imitate Donald Duck, Mickey Mouse, Alfred Hitchcock, Scooby Doo, etc. etc. etc. My own burping habits are notorious.

I believe Carly was 13, maybe 14. *She* was *third* generation annoyed with her goofy dad – eye rolls, admonitions to "grow up," general disgust. She no longer participated in the Secret Frey Handshake (the name is as much as I can say about that ... it's secret) or in the Good Bad Joke Club, in which points are awarded for making up a pun so corny, it's deemed funny.

I have sought a common ground of mutual acceptance with Carly:

"Stop being annoying, dad."
"I'll make you a deal. I won't criticize your constant giggling with your friends, you don't criticize my goofiness."
"I'm *supposed* to be like that; I'm a teenager. You're an adult."

She had me against the wall, rationally speaking, so I turned to my training as a goofy man ... new tactic:

"Dad, you're annoying me, again."
"OK. Sometimes you annoy me."
"I'm supposed to be like this, I'm 15." (Do you begin to see a pattern to her attack?).
"Welllll, there's good news and bad news."
"What?" (Ah-ha, I've drawn her into my lair).
"The bad news is that goofiness runs rampant in this family; it's your legacy and you, too, will probably never grow out of it. The good news is that you won't become a

bored, boring adult who forgets how to have fun in ways that are not always dignified."

With a noticeable lack of sincerity in her voice, Carly replied "Great."

Carly is now pushing 17. There has been no significant breakthrough in my quest to be understood and truly appreciated for the gift of inter-generational silliness I am attempting to bequeath her. However, often when we talk on the phone or I'm ready to retire for the night, she still says, "I love you" with great sincerity. Unconditional love is alive and well in the Frey family, alongside unconditional annoyance. And guess what? Carly has a burp that can raise the rafters ("you do so, Carly!") ... there's hope for the future.

39

DENIAL

(Scribner)

♦

These days, my son prefers his mother to me. I view this as a sort of cosmic re-balancing, compensating for the years when my daughter has given me her unending adoration while treating her mother like an uninvited guest at a private party.

Now I know how that feels. Susan leaves the house before the rest of us in the morning. One day recently, she kissed Daniel good-bye and went to work. Minutes later he gazed up at me and uttered two words: "Where mommy."

Grammatically, it was a question. But it was voiced more as a complaint. No, not a complaint; an *accusation*: "Where mommy."

"She just left to go to work."

"No."

"Yes ... but you'll get to see her again after work today."

"No."

"You really miss mommy when she leaves, huh?"

"Yeah."

"Need a sad hug?"

"Yeah."

He collapsed upon my chest. We felt connected. He soon turned his attention to the cartoon on TV. Then a commercial break came.

"Where mommy."

"Where *did* she go?" I challenged.

"At work."

"That's right, she's still at work."

"No."

We've been down this path before. What's called for now is distraction. I summon up three field-tested solutions: the Staged Pre-Scripted Disagreement Game, followed immediately by the Overly-Frantic Silliness Game, and concluding with my patented game, the one I've lightheartedly named "Existential Child Abuse."

I open with the requisite first move.

"She really is at work."

"Nuh-uh," he counters.

"Uh-huh." In my best taunting, playground-provocateur tone of voice.

"Nuh-uh." His eyes twinkle as he smiles, signaling his acceptance of the rules of the game.

"You're in denial."

"I not in 'nile!" Beginning to chuckle now.

"Uh-huh."

"Nuh-uh."

"You really are in denial."

"I not in 'nile. *You* in 'nile!"

"No way."

"Uh-huh – *way!*" A talented player. He caught the flaw in his delivery and self-corrected.

"No way."

"Way." Laughing fully now. Time to shift to phase two.

"Wait! I think I *do* know where your mommy is!" With each word, building tension, increasing momentum. "I'm pretty sure I saw her sneaking ... under ... the ... *couch!*" Together, we fling ourselves to the floor, laughing as we frantically search the three-inch-high space beneath the sofa. We scramble around, bumping heads, crawling over each other.

"Or maybe she climbed into ... Abby's ... *sneaker* here!" I grab the shoe, probing urgently inside it, turning it upside-down and shaking it, yelling "Mommy!" all the while. Then, I make a sad face and wail melodramatically, crying fake tears.

He comes over to comfort me with a hug, saying "Don't cry, Deeda!"

"Thank you, buddy. I feel much better now." I allow the warmth to linger for the brief time he can withstand it. When he begins to release me, I shift to the final phase: "Existential Child Abuse."

"Well, I *was* happy, but now I'm *worried!* I can't find my *Daniel* now! Where is he? Where could he be? Where did he go?"

Daniel jumps up and down directly in front of me, poking himself in the chest with his finger. "I right here! I right here!"

My eyes dart around the room, looking up, down, over him, around him, past him, behind him, everywhere but *at* him. I search frenetically, pretending not to see him. "Where *is* he? He was here just a minute ago!" I lift him up to examine the place on the floor where he was standing. "Nope ... not here either!" As I plant his feet back on the floor, he resumes jumping and pointing at himself.

He's squealing with delight now, dashing about, trying to thrust himself into my field of view as I look all around. "I right here! I right here!" We continue for several minutes. Finally, I yield. The yielding is the most important part of the game. I lock my eyes onto his.

"Oh, *there* you are! I *missed* you!" He smiles and sighs with relief. We smile some more and wipe the perspiration from our respective brows. Time for a rest break. He climbs up to join me in the big recliner, settling contentedly into my lap to watch the cartoon. Until the commercial break.

"Deeda?" Again, his tone is glum, edgy.

"Hm?"

"Where mommy?"

So, what has happened here? Did I change the unpleasant reality that he repeatedly faces – that mother sometimes goes away? No. Did I respond empathically and supportively to the feelings evoked in him? Just for a few moments here and there. Just what exactly *have* I accomplished?

I think this: I've created with him an episode in his life when father and son are together, connected, interacting, and mutually feeling happiness and joy for a while. Many a man has lamented the absence of such moments in his boyhood. I try to give Daniel some of those moments. I hope they stick with him.

And maybe, someday, he'll look up at his mother and demand: "Where Deeda."

40

HUMILITY AND VALIDATION

(Frey)

◆

I am a writer. **FatherTime** is my fourth book and I get great joy out of writing. I must also admit, however, that I am a man who has a great desire for accomplishment and, as such, I am somewhat vulnerable to the impressions of those close to me when I write. I'll admit it: my kids' opinions about me matter. I can soar to new heights or sink to new depths on the wind of their words. In the words of W.C. Fields, "allow me to elucidate":

HUMILITY

It's almost Christmas of 1994 and I have been anxiously awaiting the publication of my first book, **Double Jeopardy: Treating The Dual Disorder of Sexual Abuse And Substance Abuse**; a 2+ year process of rough drafts, an unexpected publishing deal, and the seemingly interminable wait to see one of my dreams come to fruition. I'm sitting in my office doing what I often do when not in a therapy session – avoiding paperwork (odd pastime for a writer), when the UPS guy arrives at my door bearing an early holiday surprise. "The envelope please." I open my brand spanking new first book, hot off the presses. I sit, for a long time, cradling my book, caressing the cover like it is a being I just gave birth to (longer than labor, but I make no claim of the same degree of pain or courage). I read and re-read the dedication page: *This book is dedicated to my wife, DiAnne, and my children, Carly, Aimee, and Nathan. You inspire my life.*

(Run the clock ahead a few hours) My daughters are home. I proudly carry my new creation into the house and announce the arrival of "Ta-da, **DOUBLE JEOPARDY!**"

Carly says, "Are we in it?" I read them the dedication, my heart swelling. Aimee looks into my eyes and says ... "Cool." The girls return to their activities with a robust, "So, are we going to order pizza?" On the inside I laugh and cry. I think, by day I may be Chris Frey, therapist and author extraordinaire, but off the clock I'm Dad, no more, no less. They do not know of me as a powerful healer or writer, they know me as the thrower of baseballs, renter of videos, driver of cars, hugger, listener, setter of rules ... and buyer of pizza. And so, this non-teenage netherworld in which I exist, in which we speak of trauma healing and the importance of men learning to share the truth of their feelings, of the importance of watching a hawk soar over the Missouri River, of the powerful changes I have gone through in my creative writing process; this world brings them to stare at me quizzically and with great patience utter, "Sure, dad, whatever."

I lick my wounded ego and realize that my children exist, in part, to keep me from becoming too full of myself. My most important role, father, is also my most humbling.

VALIDATION

It's the early summer of 1997 and my second book, **Men At Work: An Action Guide to Masculine Healing**, has just hit the streets to a very positive response. I am just as excited as I was at Christmas of 1994, maybe more so. **Double Jeopardy** was my first literary creation, but this new book is so close to my heart; it's about the men I've helped and it's about my life. I also receive my first copy of the new book within minutes of visiting my friend and mentor, Jackie Holler, who is only days from dying of lung cancer and to whom **Men At Work** is dedicated. It's a deeply sad and exhilarating day.

As I drive home I am reminded of my family's response to **Double Jeopardy** and, being two and a half years wiser, I am fully prepared for the reaction I believe I will receive. As expected, DiAnne is pleased, offering hugs and congrats and a celebratory bottle of sparkling apple juice. At the first opportunity, I give Carly the wonderful news and am showered with mild disinterest, although she does agree to read the book, someday, without any threats of loss of allowance. Aimee surprises me by showing a real interest in reading the book, a reminder of the little gifts I often get from my daughters, gifts given unconsciously, naturally. As this moment passes I begin to turn inward, staying connected to my own excitement, which is considerable. I truly revel in the flood of loving comments from good friends and other family members which come over the next several days.

A week or so later I awake feeling, again, quite full of myself. I'm proud of my acceptance of the girls' reaction. I'm floating along, enjoying the look, feel and sound of my new creation. I have decided that the family celebration is over and I must stay inward to enjoy a job well done and not simply move on to my next project. DiAnne goes off to work early that day and I am preparing Nathan's ritual bowl of cereal as he shakes off the grogginess of his night's sleep. Turning around and looking down, I find Nate standing in front of me with his hand out. Gazing into his open palm I see a quarter and a penny ... 26 cents. "Dad, I want to buy one of your books so I can read it." I am stunned and (quite uncharacteristically) at a loss for words. With tears in my eyes, I eke out "Sure, buddy, I'd really appreciate that. I'll bring you one home tonight."

The next morning Nathan accepts his autographed copy, making sure I pocket his payment. He leafs briefly through each page, looks me in the eye, makes his pronouncement: "Good book, dad." He stashes it on his shelf and heads off to play. I am, in that peak moment, again humbled, realizing how much I do not know about the capacity of my children to love me and the folly of attempting to predict their responses. The teacher is again taught by the child; the lesson is on how to stay in the present, to taste all of the juiciness of a remarkable time in my life; to live right here, right now.

It's a good day and I believe in that instant that I will receive no greater praise for my work than from the boy who cannot yet read.

41

JOY

(Scribner)

♦

A few years ago, I got serious about pursuing my long-dormant interest in writing. I played around with many different kinds of writing, and found light, humorous verse to be the most enjoyable.

So, I got serious about honing my skills and learning the craft of light versification. I began reading in greater depth, getting better acquainted with the masters of the form. I got serious about evaluating my own work, learning to step back from it so that I could critique it more objectively, and learning to separate my *writing* from *myself*, so that I no longer felt so vulnerable when seeking feedback from others (including my editorially-astute wife Susan, who tirelessly reads and critiques with the loving honesty that I ask for).

Then, I got serious about researching possible markets for my steadily-improving verse. I sent off for sample copies of various humor magazines and literary journals. I explored; I read; I studied. Eventually, I determined that one publication (*Light Quarterly*) stood head and shoulders above the rest.

I decided that if I was *really* serious about fashioning myself into a genuine writer of light verse, then this publication was the one I should be aiming for. I told Susan that getting one of my poems published in *that* journal would make me happier than anything I've done in years.

I selected a few of my best pieces and submitted them. Several weeks later they reappeared in my mailbox, inside the self-addressed stamped envelope I'd sent along with my submission. Attached to the poems was a small slip of paper from the editor which bore two enigmatic words: *Not Quite.*

This scenario repeated itself a few more times. I was pleased to find that I was not discouraged by the rejections; instead, I felt challenged to polish my work even more. I wrote, revised, submitted; wrote some more, revised some more, and submitted some more. I was, after all, *serious* about this pursuit.

Then, one day, it came – an acceptance letter. Upon retrieving the envelope from the mailbox, I noticed it was lighter than usual – no returned poem, just a note from the editor, who was "very pleased to accept it." My eyes lingered on that line, scanning it over again, savoring the words. Pride surged in my chest. Intense satisfaction radiated throughout my body. I was happy – seriously happy.

Susan got home soon thereafter; I wordlessly handed her the letter and watched her reaction. She let out a squeal, then congratulated me with words and a hug. I suddenly became aware of how *quietly* I celebrate things.

My daughter Abby came in next, freshly picked up from school. I told her that one of my poems was going to be published in a magazine. Her eyes grew wide as she gasped, drew in a deep breath, and began her own full-body celebration: jumping up and down, tossing her head to and fro, waving her arms in the air, chanting over and over "You're gonna be in the magazine! You're gonna be in the magazine!" Her enthusiasm was contagious, and soon I was jumping right along with her, hand in hand, chanting that joyful refrain.

Right then and there, I vowed to celebrate my future acceptances more boisterously. To date, there have been 22 of them ... and my legs haven't even *begun* to get tired yet.

Thanks, Abby, for showing me the value of not being quite so *serious* about joy.

DADS IN COMMUNITY

It no longer bothers me that I may be constantly searching for father figures; by this time, I have found several and dearly enjoyed knowing them all.

— Alice Walker

42

A HERO'S JOURNEY

(Frey)

♦

The sun is just beginning to warm the early morning as we cast our fishing lines into the water.

In truth, Jim casts into the water; I cast into the weeds, and Nathan loses interest in casting altogether and begins having a great time playing with the worms. True to his word, our friend has taken Nate and me on our first father-son fishing trip and it's way cool.

After a time, another father and his two sons pass by and prepare to fish 30 yards or so down the shore. Immediately, the day takes on a different tenor as the father lays into the older boy, who appears to be all of 10 years old: "Don't cast like that ... Are you stupid? ... You can't get anything right ... I should have left you with your mother ... Just get out of the way ... Don't be a baby!" The boy takes in the verbal battering and tries harder to please his dad. The other son simply, and wisely, is staying quiet and out of dad's (harm's) way.

I ask Jim if he can hear the father. He listens and we begin to ponder what action, if any, we should take. We fish and ponder, fish and ponder. As I continue to consider my options I see Jim drop his pole, turn and walk toward the man and his sons. He stops a safe distance away and says to the man, "Hey, did your father talk to you the way you're talking to your son?" The man's immediate response is, "As a matter of fact he did." Jim replies, "Well, maybe you could quit shaming *your* son that way." Complete silence covers the pond. Jim turns, walks back to his spot, recovers his fishing pole and casts his line into the water, under the sober gaze of the father.

Much to my surprise, the father says nothing more to Jim. Instead, he turns back to his children. Within a few minutes he is helping both of his sons learn how to cast their lines and reel in the fish they catch; there are no more shaming words, literally none. I later hear him praise the previously tormented boy on the size of his catch. After a time Jim again reels in his line and steps back toward the man and his sons. Jim asks to see their catch, compliments the boys for their efforts and makes brief, easy conversation with the father on the merits of various fishing techniques.

Later, as we leave, I see two boys smiling; three counting Nathan. In a simple act of loving confrontation, Jim has touched all of our lives. Will this father change? He already has. Will the change last? Maybe, maybe not. At the very least he has been given a better way and his sons, for moments, have seen the loving father that lives inside the man-child who scares them.

As for our little troop, we catch no fish that day, but are filled with the promise of another morning.

"Jim, can we take a boat next time?"

"Sure we can, Nate."

43

SELFISHNESS

(Scribner)

♦

It's too easy to earn the title of "good father."

If I do some laundry, or go clothes shopping with my daughter, or even make a misguided attempt to cut my son's hair (leaving him looking like a state hospital patient prepped for psychosurgery), I am applauded as having gone above and beyond the call of duty, and acknowledged as a "good father." The response echoes from countless women; "Wow, *my* husband would never do that ...."

What this tells me is that people don't expect much from fathers.

Last night, I wonder if I was such a good father. My son was sick, with an especially unpleasant illness. He was messy, restless, regressed to repeating need-driven phrases over and over, and too uncomfortable to be distracted by the usual diversions. He (and thus *we*) hadn't slept the previous night, nor this day. He was tired and fussy. *I* was tired and fussy. My wife was tired and fussy. My daughter, a heavier sleeper, was well-rested but bothered by the sudden lack of attention from her parents and brother. Weary from the day, and feeling the tug of domestic obligations, I struggled over whether to go to my men's group, which serves my goal of becoming a better father, husband, and man. I am not in the habit of skipping out on my family when the going gets tough, but this men's group has become a *very* important part of my life. In my wife's eyes, to be sure, the way to be a good husband and father *this* night would be to stay at home and be there with her, dealing with the children. I almost jumped into doing this, but the gravity of anticipatory resentment grounded me. I was on familiar turf: ignoring what is truly important and vital to me in order to meet the hopes and expectations of those around me. I realized that if I were to stay home, any care-giving I did would have been tainted, as it would be coming from a grudging sense of obligation rather than from my heart. For some people, this is no problem. For me, it's a big problem. When I'm resentful, I'm not a caring father. When I'm resentful, I'm not a loving husband. My wife made it clear to me that if I were to leave, she would be angry at me. And I knew that if I were to stay, I would be angry at myself. I've often traveled that path of compromised vitality, of living life with only half of my heart. It's like death.

Living life passionately has become important to me, especially in my role as father. I believe that "just showing up" is not enough. I've lived far too much of my life as if it *were* enough --

going along with things I only half-heartedly agreed with; remaining in situations, relationships, jobs that I'd realized long ago weren't right for me; staying home on occasions like this, giving the appearance of "fathering" when in fact I'd only be half-present, marking time until I could pursue my heart's desire.

I went to my meeting.

Later, with my evening's work completed, I returned home to give what little energy I had left to the task of caring for the sick, unsleeping child. As a "make-up" for being gone for that part of the evening, I'd agreed to do *both* parts of the parenting "graveyard shift" (midnight to 4:00 a.m. *and* 4:00 a.m. to 8:00 a.m.) instead of alternating each shift with Susan. My body was unhappy that night and the next day, but my heart and soul were in good condition. Hoping it doesn't fall on a first or third Sunday evening, I look forward to the next opportunity I'll have to show my wholeheartedness and soulfulness as a parent, a husband, and a man. In those qualities, I grew a bit last night. As I continue with that growth I notice that, despite being away from home far too many evenings, when I *am* home, I am much more fully *there*. I hope that makes up for the absences, although I'm pretty sure that in the short run my wife and children don't see it that way.

For myself, I've found that living as if I have no needs of my own is a mistake. But, doing it the other way often has difficult or unpleasant consequences which I'm obliged to face. I'm fortunate in that regard to have been blessed with a wife who is willing to support me even when she doesn't agree with me or understand me.

My son is recovering now, from both his illness and his haircut. I'm recovering from the discomfort surrounding the question of whether I did the "right" thing. I'm pretty sure I did. But for me, part of the struggle to be a good father results from having no clear guidelines on how to reconcile my own needs with the needs of others. I see men going to either extreme. I see some men who are self-absorbed, consistently giving priority to *their* needs, and their needs only. I see other men working so hard *not* to be like the men just described that they fail to take their own needs into consideration, and wind up behaving in ways that outwardly look devoted and caring, while inwardly accumulating a storehouse of resentment which is bound to express itself eventually through anger, sarcasm, or perhaps depression.

To father well, we must seek a balance -- a balance which is not easy to achieve, and which may need to be re-adjusted from day to day, or even from moment to moment.

Fathering well is demanding work.

44

BLENDING

(Frey)

♦

My daughters are "step-children." They are "children of divorce." We are a "blended family." You've seen the terminology; you've probably read about the ravages of divorce and remarriage on the psyches and community behaviors of these kids. Some doomsayers, many researchers, and the popular press have pre-destined my daughters to a life path fraught with destruction, of self and others.

And so I have waited for this impending disaster to occur. As I have waited, three other parents and I have continued to guide and love these girls. I keep running into who my children *really* are, not who the hell-fire and brimstoners of family destruction say they will be. Carly: extroverted, bright, funny, pretty, sarcastic, occasionally explosive, a funny combo of self-absorption and social worker. Aimee: introverted, voracious reader, natural intelligence, her mother's beautiful skin tone, grumpy, uncertain of her strengths, emotionally open, prone to clearly communicating her feelings about her parents' divorce. This is just some of who they are, some of what I am capable of seeing. I know they are much, much more.

I have often said to families of divorce that the choice to end a marriage, a choice in which the children have no vote, is a powerful trauma, and that each child will be wounded in ways that may not be apparent for some time. I have also often said the following: "But ... divorce is not the only major factor which will determine the health of your children. I know many children of divorce who are happy, mature, healthy people. I know many children of intact families who are a mess. What do we need to do to assist your children with the wound of your divorce? What are the other key factors in your child's life and well-being?"

Were my children wounded by my divorce? Absolutely. I have stories aplenty of the pain they have both expressed while coping with separation, remarriage, step- and half-siblings, house to house transfers. How do I know of this pain? They show me; they tell me. Expressions of anger, sadness, guilt, confusion, feelings of abandonment are not strangers to our household. Neither are listening, understanding, healing, unconditional love and joy.

Divorce alone does not doom a child to his or her own future of divorce, irresponsibility, addiction, crime, poor interpersonal relationships, and all other manner of catastrophes peddled by many of the "experts." Let me offer a list of less-publicized factors that may intervene in a child's behalf:

- My daughters have four loving, involved parents, all of whom have played a vital role in their development. My wife provides the wonderful model for step-mothers from which I teach in my counseling practice; available, loving, fun, strong. In our house the barb, "You are not my mother!" has never been spoken. Why? Because we are concerned with helping the children discover who their step-mom and step-dad *are*, rather than who they are not. In fact, the words "step-"anything are rarely spoken; we have moms and dads and brothers and sisters. We are all acutely aware of who the steps and halves are; belaboring the point serves no purpose other than creating distance between us.

- Carly and Aimee know that, all differences aside, I have an abiding respect for their mother. How could I not? I stood in awe while she brought them into this world.

- We talk about IT. At various stages of family and child development; (remarriage, new births, dating) the need arises for the all three of our children to talk about the divorce.

These moments are never planned, at least not by me. They are never easy, and they are always healing. Over the years I have learned from a little girl how to prevent a divorce. I have seen the tribulations of children moving between two households. I have heard of the guilt a teenager feels when she chooses peers over parents. The stories are varied, but the message is always the same: trauma is healed by the opportunity to express the pain in the presence of a loving, accepting significant person. Expressing the pain as it is felt prevents the storehousing of wounds that are later cashed in for greater trauma.

• There is a measure of health among the four parents. We are free of active addictions; there is no child abuse; we are involved in each child's daily life; each child is greatly loved; and each child is disciplined. We make mistakes that have no relationship to being divorced; we would have made them anyway, and in that regard our mission is no different than that of any other parent: to improve.

• Paradoxically, by divorcing and remarrying, DiAnne and I have given our children a picture of a solid, committed, joyful marriage that would not otherwise have been possible.

• We have begun to provide all of our children, especially in recent years, with what Michael Gurian (in **The Wonder of Boys**) so eloquently describes as a "Tribe"; not only parents and grandparents, but uncles, aunts, old friends and new, members of the ManKind Project and the Woman Within; a spiritual community of love and discipline for them to flourish inside of.

And so, in spite of the odds-makers, we have persevered, with much good fortune. We're an odd configuration of a family; we all know it, and we thrive within it. I refuse to deny the pain I have caused my children because of my failed marriage; we will face it, and we will heal it. There will no doubt be more pain; some of it may follow them to adulthood. The time may come when I am called to a therapist's office, not my own, but that of the person who is helping a daughter or son heal some portion of the trauma that I could not reach.

And I also refuse to accept the stigma that a teacher once, in all her well intentioned ignorance, offered to lay on our family plate: "Considering your divorce, your daughter is doing very well." As I looked at my girl's social skills, her beautiful face, her creative mind, her open heart, and her great humor, I thought, "Very well, indeed."

45

DIVERSITY

(Scribner)

♦

It's fascinating to watch Abby's awareness of diversity unfold. In our household, we strive always to view and discuss people simply *as* people. Well, we occasionally discuss *pets* as people too, noting that our cat, Harris Tweed, has a name (like us), lives in our home (like us), and is considered a member of the family (like us). Concerning Harry, my only explicit lesson to Abby about "differentness" has been that he has no thumbs, which accounts for his inability to draw, use utensils, help kids tie their shoes, etc. In most other respects, he's just one of us.

In preschool, Abby dealt with forms of diversity that mattered to her. She categorized the other children as "silly/not silly," "strong/not strong," or "knows the names of all the shapes/doesn't know them." Only later did she begin to distinguish kids by their physical characteristics. Her views on racial diversity were beautiful in their simplicity. She described her various classmates as having "red hair and blue eyes," "black hair and white skin," and "brown eyes and brown skin."

One day she went to play at a friend's house. This friend is the child of a bi-racial couple. Upon returning home, Abby told me all about the play-date, the things they did, the toys her friend had. Then she offhandedly mentioned "and I got to meet Katie's brother. He has skin just like hers."

"*Just* like hers?" I replied, with mock astonishment. "You mean it covers his *whole* body, just like hers, and yours, and mine?"

"No, Deeda," she smiled. "That same kind of tan color. Her mom's skin is just kinda white. But Katie and her brother both have tan skin."

"So, what do you think about that?" I asked.

"I liked it. I wish mine was that color."

A few months later, now in kindergarten, Abby had just gotten home from the class Halloween party. Her mother and I had been there, too, to help with the party. Several other moms, and a smattering of dads, also attended. Smugly, I noticed that Abby was the only child who had *both* parents there. Hoping that she too had noticed, I pulled for a bit of acknowledgment.

"So, what did you think about having your parents in your classroom today?"

My imagination scripted this response: *Father, I was so pleased that both you and Mother took time off work to be present. It truly demonstrates the depth of your love for me, and that depth is surpassed only by the depth of my gratitude to you for being there.*

Abby gave this response: "Good."

Evidently, she was put on this Earth to teach me that indirect communication just doesn't cut it.

She continued. "James' mom was there, and her skin is the same color as his."

"Why do you suppose that is?" I asked, ever on the lookout to correct any budding misconceptions she might have.

"James says it's because they're African-American." Apparently, she had taken it upon herself to investigate the matter independently.

Abby has gotten interested in basketball, and she now enjoys watching games with me. She has grasped the concepts of trying to make the ball go into the basket, dribbling with the ball rather than running with it, and the general principle of "defense." She enjoys practicing counting by twos whenever a basket is made. She constantly asks questions and makes comments about what is happening on the screen as she watches. The theme that seems to organize much of her perceptiveness these days arose again recently.

"Deeda, a lot of the basketball players have brown skin."

I acknowledged the validity of her observation. "What do you think of that?" I asked.

"I think they must be African-American."

After seeing the movie *Space Jam*, Abby became a big Michael Jordan fan. Every time a player on TV got the ball, she would excitedly ask "is *that* Michael Jordan?" If the answer is *"no"* she insists on learning what the player's name is. She likes learning new words, including new names, and the NBA offers a rich assortment. Watching the NBA All-Star Game, the first two players she asked about happened to be Hakeem Olajuwan and Dikembe Mutumbo. She asked me to repeat each name, unsure that she'd heard me correctly. "They have funny names," she commented.

I explained that both men are from Africa, and that in Africa as in most other places, people have names that sound different from the names of most people in America – just as different countries have different-sounding languages. She accepted that.

She's developing a clear *awareness* of diversity, including racial diversity – but I've been pleased to see that that's where it ends for her. She observes, takes note of obvious distinctions, and that's that. No evaluations. No judgments. No stereotypes. I like what I'm seeing. I hope it continues.

Last week I was driving Abby to school and I popped in a cassette, filling the car with the soulful

Texas twang of Lyle Lovett. Abby has told me she likes his music. This time, it sparks her curiosity.

"Deeda, is Lyle Lovett white? Or is he African-American?"

"He's white. Why do you ask?"

"Well, he sorta sounds like he's African-American."

The vagaries of regional accents and country-blues diction will be lessons for some other day. For now, I just nodded.

46

FATHERS AND WIVES

(Scribner)

◆

My wife is bothered that the pieces I'm writing for this book don't often mention her. "A woman would never write a book about parenting without focusing on the other person involved, too," she says. It sounds like she's feeling unappreciated, feeling like I don't notice *her* parenting talents, all the energy *she* devotes to her own growth as a parent, and all the parenting she does do.

"Are you feeling unappreciated, or like I don't notice or acknowledge all that *you* do as a parent?" I ask.

She replies "I feel like you notice on a day-to-day basis, but I just wish that would inspire you to write about it, too."

So, she knows that I do appreciate her as a parent, and as my parenting partner – but she wants to see that in print.

Well, Susan, here it is:

You are a tremendous mother. You help make **me** a better parent by helping me recognize the importance of balancing my frequent periods of self-absorption with a greater awareness of the needs and feelings of others. **You** are the one doing much of the parenting work, there in the trenches with our children, parenting solo all those evenings that I'm at work. **You** are the one who is always on top of "*who* has *what* event on *which* day," *when* the teacher-conference is, *what* family outings need to happen this week. And **you** deserve special credit for your desire and willingness to **do the work** of pursuing continued growth as a parent, and remaining committed to that process. I honor you, I admire you, I love you, and I cannot imagine a better person to have as my parenting partner.

There it is, in print, for all to see. And every word of it is true.

Now, why *have* I been focusing so much on me and my fathering role, without speaking much of my parenting partner, my wife of 11 years?

In part, because it is important to me to claim my fathering efforts as my own, as something distinct from my wife's *mothering* efforts. In part, it's because my purpose here is to highlight that part of parenting that is the *father's*, to examine that ingredient in hopes of learning more about it. Yes, that ingredient will be blended with the mothering ingredient in order to make that cake that we call parenting. But ingredients change when they're combined, and once they're blended, it's often difficult to discern the original ingredients any more.

A father benefits from having an identity as a father that's independent of his identity as a co-parent with his wife. Fathers and mothers have unique contributions to make as parents, and part of our aim in this book is to build an awareness and recognition of the piece that is unique to fathering. How do I know that uniqueness exists?

Easy. "Okay, men ... a show of hands ... how many of you interact differently with your kids when your wife is around, compared to when it's just you and them?" When it's just *me* parenting my children, I'm less prone to "evaluate" what I'm doing, and I'm more fully-immersed in *doing* it. I'm more spontaneous. I'm more natural, fathering more from a gut sense of what to do. When Susan is around, something about her mere presence leads me to be more tentative, to second-guess myself. I don't think it's because of anything she does; it's just that knowing I'm a co-parent rather than *the* parent at that moment somehow changes me. When it's just me and the kids, I'm more wacky. I come up with ways to occupy them that I'd never try if Susan were there. I become more child-like myself, and less self-conscious. I have an easier time meeting them at their level when it's just them and me. A prominent feature of my fathering style is connecting with kids through nonsense and silliness. My children (as well as their friends) unanimously regard me as "funny," "silly," or "weird," depending on their level of tolerance for such behavior from an adult male. This is *my* way of connecting with them; it works for me. But I'm much less that way when Susan is around. The whimsy doesn't disappear completely, but I definitely tone it down.

Ideally, parenting is a joint venture. But fathers aren't really in a position to be part of that joint venture until they've gotten clear on their identity as a father -- and many of us struggle long and hard to define that identity in a healthy way. And, for better or for worse, we men often prefer (or even need) to go through those struggles independently, or in the company of other men.

Unless a father actively strives to define his role and identity as a father, he's at risk of becoming an "assistant mother" rather than a father. Not that there's any shame in being a mother. It's just that being a mother is different from being a father. The roles are distinct, unique. And equally necessary. But only in the role of father can a man bloom in his full glory as a parent.

Consider this football analogy: An accomplished and thoughtful halfback writes a book on the theory and technique of head-fakes, cradling the ball, and cutting back against the flow of the play. He might offer dozens of tips, observations, and ideas that could help the reader become a better running back. That author's wife might raise the valid point that "if it weren't for the offensive line pulling together and working as a coordinated unit, none of these fancy moves would count for diddley." Sure. But it's equally true that if the running back devoted his energies to appreciating and perhaps even emulating the offensive linemen, there might be no one to run through those wonderful gaps that the linemen create. A halfback can learn a lot about blocking and trapping by watching and emulating the offensive tackle. But doing so isn't likely to make him a better running back.

The skills and roles required are different -- and complementary. Certainly, having both a mother's voice and a father's voice is beneficial. Mothers have motherly ways of doing things. Fathers play differently with their children. They handle children's conflicts differently... And they write books differently.

By the way, Susan -- I do love and appreciate you for mothering our children as you do. And that very sentence reveals another way of recognizing the difference between being a mother and being a father: the phrase "she 'mothered' him" has a complex blend of meanings -- *loving, nurturing, doting, caring,* perhaps even *spoiling.* Any native English-speaker grasps what the phrase "mothering him" means. It's a very rich phrase, with multiple layers of significance.

In contrast, "he 'fathered' him" usually means little other than "providing a genetic contribution to offspring." THAT bothers me. My hope is that this book will contribute to a richer conception of what the distinctive job of fathering is all about -- if you'll pardon the pun.

47

OPPORTUNITY KNOCKS

(Frey)

♦

I am a divorced father of two beautiful, funny, creative, strong willed daughters. I have often thought about, and felt deep pain about, the heartache I have caused my girls as a divorced father. As a man and a therapist who deeply believes in the presence of fathers in family life, I have often, in times past, focused heavily on the *responsibilities* of being the best divorced father I can be – making phone calls, sending cards, attending school events, zealously guarding our time together. In spite of all my efforts, I have missed the first fish caught, the first successful bubble-gum bubble, the first day wearing makeup.

As the years have marched on, I've slowly become aware that the style of fathering I had adopted, within the realities of our family makeup, lacked a certain something in the joy department. As I had begun to ponder this awareness, a flu bug provided me with a valuable lesson one fine winter's night.

Aimee, who is 14 at the time of this writing, was sick with the stomach flu. You know, the one with projectiles of things you wish you hadn't eaten shooting from your body. Aim (as I have called her for years, no pun intended) has always been known in our house as "The Chronicler of Disaster"; her keen memory catalogues each family illness, mishap, accident and faux pas, providing hours of vivid stories of the type that only improve with age and re-telling. This night would soon lend itself well to the family diary.

As is the custom in our house when the flu strikes, I moved Aimee to the sofa and fetched the requisite extra pillows, clear liquids, and large bowl. I positioned Aimee at one end of the sofa and myself at the other, and we attempted to settle down for a long winter's nap, interrupted throughout the night by bouts with the bowl. The eruptions were many and the night was long. As first light appeared Sunday morning Aimee roused again, feeling somewhat better, and asked for a drink. I too awoke, with my "I'm a loving dad and I'm hyper-alert 'cause I've got a sick kid" alarm fully operational. I stood up, groaning, while she looked at me with a bleary-eyed smile and said, "Dad, do you know how many times I threw up last night?"

I sighed. "No, Aimee, how many?" I smiled back, feeling sure she knew.

"Seven, dad, seven times."

"Wow."

Now, for years I have led weekend retreats, and as anyone who has facilitated marathon group therapy experiences will tell you, mild sleep deprivation can wither the emotional defenses around your heart. In much the same way, in this odd moment with Aimee, my heart swelled, I became tearful, and I thanked God for the opportunity to be the parent who, this time, held the bowl all seven times. In that precious instant, I had a strange sort of spiritual awakening; I understood with total clarity the difference between being a loving, good dad and being a man who loved *being a dad*; I understood the difference between loving my children and *loving my opportunity to father them*. For me, and for many men, this moment is a revelation.

Today, when I am away from my children, I miss them not so much because we are apart, but because of what we are together. I miss the opportunities, and so, have a much greater appreciation for the chances to father that we do create. I enjoy, and remember, the firsts that I am present for. I have more fun, I *am* more fun, and even my adolescent daughters would probably admit they like spending time with me ... when it works into their schedules.

I carry my daughters with me always, in my heart's memory. Thank you, Aimee.

THE BIGGER PICTURE

Once you bring life into the world, you must protect it. We must protect it by changing the world.

– Elie Wiesel

48

REINCARNATION

(Frey)

♦

I was reading a wonderful book on spirituality, Sam Keen's **Hymns To An Unknown God.** Nathan, who was five at the time of this writing, asked me what I was reading that could possibly capture my interest more than the prospect of playing Legos with him. I told him it was a book about God. He said, "Oh yeah, my other mother, before I lived with you, read me that book."

You see, Nathan claims that in a previous life he lived on a farm, had what was apparently an excellent family life, and then after spending some time hanging out with God in the sky, he chose his mother and me for his next life. I'm impressed by his message to us, and although I'm not totally clear on the meaning, it seems to be a vote of confidence that we are the next step in his evolution from what was already a pretty good set of parents. More than this, I'm impressed with his origins. It occurs to me that folks who claim to be reincarnated usually recall past lives as queens, saints, emperors, poets and the like ... my son was a farmer from a healthy, happy family. And he's already met God in the most personal of ways. Me too. I've met God through the heart and story of this child. Good work, God.

49

FATHERS' RIGHTS

(Frey)

♦

I received a call today from a man I know well. A good man. He was living what was, in his best recall, his saddest day. A judge had, in all his arrogance, pounded a gavel this day and given permission to the former wife of this man to leave the state, forever, with their children. This decision was not made because the father is one of the uninvolved, "deadbeat dads" that we hear so much about; he is a good father who strives to meet his responsibilities to his children emotionally, financially, and spiritually. This decision was not driven by any urgent need in the best interests of the children; there was no catastrophic health situation, no critical financial situation on the mother's part. This decision was made *because* a mother and a judge do not truly value the essential, consistent presence of this father in his children's lives over other matters of convenience. As a therapist who cares deeply about families, I am sad. As a man and a divorced father, I am angry.

This decision was made by a man in our judicial system, a system that will spend hundreds of thousands of dollars this year pursuing and prosecuting men who don't pay their child support, who don't meet their responsibilities. Our legal system will judge and sentence to jail thousands of young criminals whose introduction to the world of masculinity was being abandoned or abused by fathers. This system will flounder in its attempts to assist droves of children without fathers who are being initiated into gangs by other, older children without fathers. We are surrounded by data from research and the media that vividly portrays the costs and risks to children of absent fathers. But today, a man who is called upon to serve our system with fairness and justice told a good father, an active father, a loving father that *his* daily presence was unnecessary, that his consistent absence was a legal mandate.

In my imagination I see this same judge, weeks or months down the road, sitting on his bench looking down at an irresponsible, uncaring father brought before him in a custody or support hearing. The judge will chastise this man for not fulfilling his commitments as a father, perhaps fine or jail him. This same judge, who may himself be a good father, will carefully avoid remembering a man he so recently sent away from the court empty handed, a man willing to fulfill those commitments. If the judge does allow himself to remember, I hope sleep does not come easy to him that night.

Are there other sides to this story? Several: the mom's, who undoubtedly also loves her children; the judge's, whose reasoning I have no interest in. Today, I am not concerned with the big picture; I'm concerned with one father and his children.

Will these children survive? Most assuredly, they will, in part with the father's continued efforts to be as involved as possible in their lives. Today, I'm concerned with the distance put between this man and these children as they attempt to *thrive*.

Today, I'm a father whose heart is with a man judged by our courts to be an inconvenience in the life plan of his children's mother, and thus, a footnote in his children's daily lives. Don't you believe it, friend, your children surely won't.

50

SONS AND WARRIORS

(Frey)

♦

I was watching a re-run of "Glory" on the tube today. It's the story of the 54th Calvary, which I believe was the first African-American regiment in the Civil War. In the last scene, as the men march through the sand to their deaths, I found myself crying for my gender, African-American men and men of all colors long dead. I was deep in my grief over the courage and foolishness of young soldiers when into the room march Nathan and his buddy Jacob decked out as make-shift superheroes. Challenging me to a duel to the death, the two mighty mites attack without provocation. Making up in stamina for what they lacked in strength; they wore me down to unconditional surrender. After the battle, we had lemon drops.

Later that evening, I could not erase the horrific, brain numbing thought of losing a son or daughter to war. As a grateful loser in the final Selective Service draft lottery, I have not been to war, and have never carried a gun, much less fired one at another human. As a therapist with men, I have mourned the sons of other men alongside soldiers who return from the war with their memories and their pain; but I've never sent a son or daughter to die for me and mine. As I wrestled to grasp an anguish I have not lived, I wrote this:

Standing on wet sand
One foot in the tears,
Of brothers long dead
Wave after wave
Littered the shoreline
With courage
And pain

A son,
Intruding upon imagination
And sorrow
Makes the men
more
real

Coming forth in,
Full regalia
Baby blanket
Turned hero's cape
Performing an ancient dance
Of challenge,
To battle

Later,
Licking the wounds
Of one more mock defeat
I imagine sons, oceans of sons, every father's son

Lost to the whims
Of foolish bullies
Trying to pull gold stars from the sky,
To arrogantly wear on their dark shirted shoulders

And I wonder,
What is the good fight?

Some wars are fought for freedom, ideals, or family; the men of the 54th Calvary must have been fighting for all of those, and for dignity. George Washington, Nelson Mandela, Martin Luther King, and Ghandi fought these wars. Sadly, though, it seems as if few of the wars in my lifetime were fought for the values embodied by these men. Rather, most wars take me back in time to the playground – a bully strutting his stuff, having something to prove and lacking any sense of reason, facing off against someone foolish enough or pushed deep enough into the corner to fight back. The critical difference between the two pictures is that my playground bully had a much smaller arsenal than the dark kings and queens, generals and presidents of my children's world.

The travelling Vietnam Veteran Memorial Wall came through our town again. I remember that each of the names on that wall is a son or daughter. I continue to labor with this writing after visiting that monument to pain and courage and love. Perhaps as a result of this labor, I have decided that I should only send my children to war after I have spent more time with the fathers of those who went to war and did not return. And perhaps I should only send my children to war after I have met the father of an *enemy*, a young man or woman who will fight for the other cause. I'll watch this father's face as he describes the birth of his child. I'll listen to the dreams that he holds for his child's future. Then, when I truly understand what war may cost not only me, but this other man, *then* maybe I will presume to send my son or daughter off to die for my freedom. Or perhaps I'll simply get better at teaching peace.

51

A DAUGHTER'S VIEW

(Frey)

♦

As I prepared to write this book, I invited Carly and Aimee to put pen to paper with their views on fathering. Carly declined, commenting that she is a talker, not a writer; I can attest to her strengths with the spoken word and supported her decision. Aimee, however, offered two essays, contained in my Father's Day card. Both are printed below, unedited except for a couple of typos. I was honored by "The Role of Fatherhood." I was amazed by the wisdom of the woman-child who wrote "Father and Son":

THE ROLE OF FATHERHOOD

I'm not a father and never will be because I'm a woman, but you can't have a father like mine and not gather this information. To be a good father the following are all the qualities:

A father must respect his children if he wants to be respected. It is impossible to show respect if it isn't shown back.

A father is someone who is always there to listen to you when you need him; however big or small the problem may be to him, it may mean a lot to you.

A father is understanding, but being understanding doesn't mean no discipline. If you discipline your kids they may thank you in the long run no matter how many times they said they'd never forgive you.

A father must be supportive. Young or old your child will always need parental support (even if they don't ask for it or show you they need it).

Above all, a father must be a good role model for a son or daughter. A child must have someone positive to look up to. That is one of the most important rules of parenting because however your children see you, they will be the same for their kids. Role models are most important in a child's life.

So, to be a good father just make sure you understand everything written above. I'm only 15 and you're probably thinking, "What would she know," but I know all this to be true because of my father, Chris. Everything written is what he is, especially a role model.

Just remember to do all the things I've written and your children will thank you for being there for them when they needed you.

BY: AIMEE FREY, 1998

FATHER AND SON

I'm only 15 years old and I've decided I want to be an author. Well, when my dad, Chris Frey, gave me the opportunity to write something for his book, I took it seriously.

I've been watching my dad and my 6 year old brother; they interact well together.

232

Through my observations of not just my dad and brother, but other fathers and sons, too, this is what I think the stages of sons growing up are:

During childhood, the son looks up to his father. He wants to be exactly like his father and the father couldn't be happier. Then Stage 2 comes (the rebellious stage).

As the son gets older, he starts to get more distant and needs more space. The father isn't upset, though, because he knows it's for the best.

Stage 3 is when the son gets older still and is still distant and starts to go his own way (college, job, home). In other words, he is an adult. The father is supportive throughout this.

The Fourth Stage is the final stage. That is the stage when the son becomes a father. It is also when the father and son start to bond and get close again.

My point is that throughout all stages, the father is basically always supportive. They may disagree, but he stays supportive. Also, the son may not think he looks up to his father, but he does. He just doesn't realize it.

In conclusion, those are my theories of the father and son relationship. But, the son is not the only one with these same stages. A daughter will also go through them. I would know because I'm still going through them, myself.

BY: AIMEE FREY, 1998

52

THE NEXT GENERATION

(Frey)

♦

I have a hidden storehouse of songs, written by yours truly. Of all that I write – essays, books, poems – I am the least secure in my songs. They are from my heart; they are often sad, and they are sometimes syrupy, reminding me of the music I hear on the radio just before I change the station. Below you will find the first song that I have written that has ever seen the light of day ... or at least the light outside of my living room. It is fitting that the song is not about me, it's about *us* ... fathers. Perhaps this is what allows me to climb out of myself long enough to share the lyrics with you:

As the light comes down on fatherhood
As the time of need has passed
As the childhood voices come of age
Has he fashioned dreams to last

Was his wakefulness a guiding fire
Was his love the touch of Kings
Did he teach enough of miracles
Gift a sacred song to sing

So he stands alone, his watchful eyes
Turned out to the West
And he cries the tears of setting suns
And knows he has been blessed

Then, the dawn taps on his shoulder
The life force from the East
Sending promises of new creation
The cub, the sapling
Spring's mountain stream
A son or daughter
A man redeemed
He lives forever
In the Father's dream
The circle is complete

He lives forever
In the Father's dream
The circle is complete

A simple song, from the heart.

53

WHEN DOES THE NEED FOR ALL THIS EFFORT AND SELF-AWARENESS END?

♦

Never. But if you keep at it, it eventually ceases to be such a chore. So, once you're doing it, don't forget to lighten up.

CONCLUSION

We have not inherited the earth from our fathers; we are borrowing it from our children.

— Native American saying

As **FatherTime** comes to a close, the stories continue. Some will be written; some will simply remain etched in our memories. Our intention, and our hope for you as well, is that as we create new stories we will come to fully appreciate the significance of our lives as fathers.

We hope you've found a piece of what you were looking for in these pages. And we hope that, as a dad, you've taken these messages to heart:

- *We are better fathers when we attend to our own inner journeys.*

- *We help ourselves, our children, and the world when we create a community of men, women and children to support, teach and nurture us.*

- *We fathers are often at our best when we are "doers"; be a father of loving action.*

- *We fathers have undertaken an adventure that is both emotional and spiritual; be mindful of its significance.*

Care for your children, love them, and have fun with them. And keep doing whatever you need to do on your *own* journey to make all of that possible.

How to Contact the Authors:

We welcome your comments about this book; please let us know what you think.

CHRISTOPHER SCRIBNER:
Insight Output, P.O. Box 1944, St. Louis, MO 63043
314/434-2889
insight@i1.net

CHRIS FREY:
Frey & Tobin Counseling Associates, 10918 Olive
Boulevard, Creve Coeur, MO 63141
314/997-1403
freyeagle@prodigy.net

Chris Frey's other titles are also available; contact him at the address above.
- *Men At Work: An Action Guide To Masculine Healing*
- *Double Jeopardy: Treating Juveniles For The Dual Disorder Of Sexual Abuse And Substance Abuse*

Chris Scribner's poetry and humorous prose frequently appear in:

> *Light: The Quarterly of Light Verse*
> (Box 7500, Chicago, IL, 60680)
>   and
> *Journal of Irreproducible Results*
> (P.O. Box 234, Chicago Heights, IL, 60411)

Order extra copies of

FATHERTIME

for fathers, fathers-to-be, friends, or your local library

Quantity discounts available:

1-9 copies	$14.95 each
10-24 copies	$12.95 each
25+ copies	$10.50 each

Shipping and Handling:
$3.00 first book; $1.50 each book thereafter.

Quantity	Unit Price	Amount
MO residents add 6.475% sales tax		
Shipping & Handling		
TOTAL		

Make check payable to :

INSIGHT OUTPUT
P.O. Box 1944
St. Louis, MO 63043

(For shipping to countries outside the U.S., please inquire).